Contents

INTRODUCTION
The Roseto Mystery
"These people were dying of old age. That's it."

PART ONE: OPPORTUNITY

ONE
The Matthew Effect
"For unto everyone that hath shall be given, and he shall have
abundance. But from him that hath not shall be taken away even that
which he hath." — Matthew 25:29

TWO
The 10,000-Hour Rule
"In Hamburg, we had to play for eight hours."

THREE
The Trouble with Geniuses, Part 1
"Knowledge of a boy's IQ is of little help if you are faced with a
formful of clever boys."

FOUR
The Trouble with Geniuses, Part 2
"After protracted negotiations, it was agreed that Robert would be put
on probation."

FIVE
The Three Lessons of Joe Flom
"Mary got a quarter."

PART TWO: LEGACY

SIX
Harlan, Kentucky
"Die like a man, like your brother did!"

SEVEN
The Ethnic Theory of Plane Crashes
"Captain, the weather radar has helped us a lot ."

EIGHT
Rice Paddies and Math Tests
"No one who can rise before dawn three hundred sixty days a year
fails to make his family rich."

NINE
Marita's Bargain
"All my friends now are from KIPP."

INTRODUCTION

The Roseto Mystery

"THESE PEOPLE WERE DYING OF OLD AGE. THA T'S IT".

out·li·er \-,lī(-ə)r\ *noun*
1: something that is situated away from or classed differently from a main or related body
2: a statistical observation that is markedly different in value from the others of the sample

1.

Roseto Valfortore lies one hundred miles southeast of Rome in the Apennine foothills of the Italian province of Foggia. In the style of medieval villages, the town is organized around a large central square. Facing the square is the Palazzo Marchesale, the palace of the Saggese family, once the great landowner of those parts. An archway to one side leads to a church, the Madonna del Carmine—Our Lady of Mount Carmine. Narrow stone steps run up the hillside, flanked by closely clustered two-story stone houses with red-tile roofs.

For centuries, the *paesani* of Roseto worked in the marble quarries in the surrounding hills, or cultivated the fields in the terraced valley below, walking four and five miles down the mountain in the morning and then making the long journey back up the hill at night. Life was hard. The townsfolk were barely literate and desperately poor and without much hope for economic betterment until word reached Roseto at the end of the nineteenth century of the land of opportunity across the ocean.

In January of 1882, a group of eleven Rosetans—ten men and one boy—set sail for New York. They spent their first night in America sleeping on the floor of a tavern on Mulberry Street, in Manhattan's Little Italy. Then they ventured west, eventually finding jobs in a slate quarry ninety miles west of the city near the town of Bangor, Pennsylvania. The following year, fifteen Rosetans left Italy for America, and several members of that group ended up in Bangor as well, joining their compatriots in the slate quarry. Those immigrants, in turn, sent word back to Roseto about the promise of the New World, and soon one group of Rosetans after another packed their bags and headed for Pennsylvania, until the initial stream of immigrants became a flood. In 1894 alone, some twelve hundred Rosetans applied for passports to America, leaving entire streets of their old village abandoned.

The Rosetans began buying land on a rocky hillside connected to Bangor by a steep, rutted wagon path. They built closely clustered two-story stone houses with slate roofs on narrow streets running up and down the hillside. They built a church and called it Our Lady of Mount Carmel and named the main street, on which it stood, Garibaldi Avenue, after the great hero of Italian unification. In the beginning, they called their town New Italy. But they soon changed it to Roseto, which seemed only appropriate given that almost all of them had come from the same village in Italy.

In 1896, a dynamic young priest by the name of Father Pasquale de Nisco took over at Our Lady of Mount Carmel. De Nisco set up spiritual societies and organized festivals. He encouraged the townsfolk to clear the land and plant onions, beans, potatoes, melons, and fruit trees in the long backyards behind their houses. He gave out seeds and bulbs. The town came to life. The Rosetans began raising pigs in their backyards and growing grapes for homemade wine. Schools, a park, a convent, and a cemetery were built. Small shops and bakeries and restaurants and bars opened along Garibaldi Avenue. More than a dozen factories sprang up making blouses for the garment trade. Neighboring Bangor was largely Welsh and English, and the next town over was overwhelmingly German, which meant—given the fractious relationships between the English and Germans and Italians in those years—that Roseto stayed strictly for Rosetans. If you had wandered up and down the streets of Roseto in Pennsylvania in the first few decades after 1900, you would have heard only Italian, and not just any Italian but the precise southern Foggian dialect spoken back in the Italian Roseto. Roseto, Pennsylvania, was its own tiny, self-sufficient world—all but unknown by the society around it—and it might well have remained so but for a man named Stewart Wolf.

Wolf was a physician. He studied digestion and the stomach and taught in the medical school at the University of Oklahoma. He spent his summers on a farm in Pennsylvania, not far from Roseto—although that, of course, didn't mean much, since Roseto was so much in its own world that it was possible to live in the next town and never know much about it. "One of the times when we were up there for the summer—this would have been in the late nineteen fifties—I was invited to give a talk at the local medical society," Wolf said years later in an interview. "After the talk was over, one of the local doctors invited me to have a beer. And while we were having a drink, he said, 'You know, I've been practicing for seventeen years. I get patients from all over, and I rarely find anyone from Roseto under the age of sixty-five with heart disease.' "

Wolf was taken aback. This was the 1950s, years before the advent of cholesterol-lowering drugs and aggressive measures to prevent heart disease. Heart attacks were an epidemic in the United States. They were the leading cause of death in men under the age of sixty-five. It was impossible to be a doctor, common sense said, and not see heart disease.

Wolf decided to investigate. He enlisted the support of some of his students and colleagues from Oklahoma. They gathered together the death certificates from residents of the town, going back as many years as they could. They analyzed physicians' records. They took medical histories and constructed family genealogies. "We got busy," Wolf said. "We decided to do a preliminary study. We started in nineteen sixty-one. The mayor said, 'All my sisters are going to help you.' He had four sisters. He said, 'You can have the town council room.' I said, 'Where are you going to have council meetings?' He said, 'Well, we'll postpone them for a while.' The ladies would bring us lunch. We had little booths where we could take blood, do EKGs. We were there for four weeks. Then I talked with the authorities. They gave us the school for the summer. We invited the entire population of Roseto to be tested."

The results were astonishing. In Roseto, virtually no one under fifty-five had died of a heart attack or showed any signs of heart disease. For men over sixty-five, the death rate from heart disease in Roseto was roughly half that of the United States as a whole. The death rate from all causes in Roseto, in fact, was 30 to 35 percent lower than expected.

Wolf brought in a friend of his, a sociologist from Oklahoma named John Bruhn, to help him. "I hired medical students and sociology grad students as interviewers, and in Roseto we went house to house and talked to every person aged twenty-one and over," Bruhn remembers. This happened more than fifty years ago, but Bruhn still had a sense of amazement in his voice as he described what they found. "There was no suicide, no alcoholism, no drug addiction, and very little crime. They didn't have anyone on welfare. Then we looked at peptic ulcers. They didn't have any of those either. These people were dying of old age. That's it."

Wolf's profession had a name for a place like Roseto—a place that lay outside everyday experience, where the normal rules did not apply. Roseto was an *outlier.*

2.

Wolf's first thought was that the Rosetans must have held on to some dietary practices from the Old World that left them healthier than other Americans. But he quickly realized that wasn't true. The Rosetans were cooking with lard instead of with the much healthier olive oil they had used back in Italy. Pizza in Italy was a thin crust with salt, oil, and perhaps some tomatoes, anchovies, or onions. Pizza in Pennsylvania was bread dough plus sausage, pepperoni, salami, ham, and sometimes eggs. Sweets such as biscotti and *taralli* used to be reserved for Christmas and Easter; in Roseto they were eaten year-round. When Wolf had dieticians analyze the typical Rosetan's eating habits, they found that a whopping 41 percent of their calories came from fat. Nor was this a town where people got up at dawn to do yoga and run a brisk six miles. The Pennsylvanian Rosetans smoked heavily and many were struggling with obesity.

If diet and exercise didn't explain the findings, then what about genetics? The Rosetans were a close-knit group from the same region of Italy, and Wolf's next thought was to wonder whether they were of a particularly hardy stock that protected them from disease. So he tracked down relatives of the Rosetans who were living in other parts of the United States to see if they shared the same remarkable good health as their cousins in Pennsylvania. They didn't.

He then looked at the region where the Rosetans lived. Was it possible that there was something about living in the foothills of eastern Pennsylvania that was good for their health? The two closest towns to Roseto were Bangor, which was just down the hill, and Nazareth, a few miles away. These were both about the same size as Roseto, and both were populated with the same kind of hardworking European immigrants. Wolf combed through both towns' medical records. For men over sixty-five, the death rates from heart disease in Nazareth and Bangor were three times that of Roseto. Another dead end.

What Wolf began to realize was that the secret of Roseto wasn't diet or exercise or genes or location. *It had to be Roseto itself.* As Bruhn and Wolf walked around the town, they figured out why. They looked at how the Rosetans visited one another, stopping to chat in Italian on the street, say, or cooking for one another in their backyards. They learned about the extended family clans that underlay the town's social structure. They saw how many homes had three generations living under one roof, and how much respect grandparents commanded. They went to mass at Our Lady of Mount Carmel and saw the unifying and calming effect of the church. They counted twenty-two separate civic organizations in a town of just under two thousand people. They picked up on the particular egalitarian ethos of the community, which discouraged the wealthy from flaunting their success and helped the unsuccessful obscure their failures.

In transplanting the *paesani* culture of southern Italy to the hills of eastern Pennsylvania, the Rosetans had created a powerful, protective social structure capable of insulating them from the pressures of the modern world. The Rosetans were healthy because of where they were *from*, because of the world they had created for themselves in their tiny little town in the hills.

"I remember going to Roseto for the first time, and you'd see three-generational family meals, all the bakeries, the people walking up and down the street, sitting on their porches talking to each other, the blouse mills where the women worked during the day, while the men worked in the slate quarries," Bruhn said. "It was magical."

When Bruhn and Wolf first presented their findings to the medical community, you can imagine the kind of skepticism they faced. They went to conferences where their peers were presenting long rows of data arrayed in complex charts and referring to this kind of gene or that kind of physiological process, and they themselves were talking instead about the mysterious and magical benefits of people stopping to talk to one another on the street and of having three generations under one roof. Living a long life, the conventional wisdom at the time said, depended to a great extent on who we were—that is, our genes. It depended on the decisions we made—on what we chose to eat, and how much we chose to exercise, and how effectively we were treated by the medical system. No one was used to thinking about health in terms of *community*.

Wolf and Bruhn had to convince the medical establishment to think about health and heart attacks in an entirely new way: they had to get them to realize that they wouldn't be able to understand why someone was healthy if all they did was think about an individual's personal choices or actions in isolation. They had to look *beyond* the individual. They had to understand the culture he or she was a part of, and who their friends and families were, and what town their families came from. They had to appreciate the idea that the values of the world we inhabit and the people we surround ourselves with have a profound effect on who we are.

In *Outliers*, I want to do for our understanding of success what Stewart Wolf did for our understanding of health.

PART ONE

OPPORTUNITY

CHAPTER ONE

The Matthew Effect

"FOR UNTO EVERYONE THAT HATH SHALL BE GIVEN, AND HE SHALL HAVE ABUNDANCE. BUT FROM HIM THAT HATH NOT SHALL BE TAKEN AWAY EVEN THAT WHICH HE HATH."—MATTHEW 25:29

1.

One warm, spring day in May of 2007, the Medicine Hat Tigers and the Vancouver Giants met for the Memorial Cup hockey championships in Vancouver, British Columbia. The Tigers and the Giants were the two finest teams in the Canadian Hockey League, which in turn is the finest junior hockey league in the world. These were the future stars of the sport—seventeen-, eighteen-, and nineteen-year-olds who had been skating and shooting pucks since they were barely more than toddlers.

The game was broadcast on Canadian national television. Up and down the streets of downtown Vancouver, Memorial Cup banners hung from the lampposts. The arena was packed. A long red carpet was rolled out on the ice, and the announcer introduced the game's dignitaries. First came the premier of British Columbia, Gordon Campbell. Then, amid tumultuous applause, out walked Gordie Howe, one of the legends of the game. "Ladies and gentlemen," the announcer boomed. "Mr. Hockey!"

For the next sixty minutes, the two teams played spirited, aggressive hockey. Vancouver scored first, early in the second period, on a rebound by Mario Bliznak. Late in the second period, it was Medicine Hat's turn, as the team's scoring leader, Darren Helm, fired a quick shot past Vancouver's goalie, Tyson Sexsmith. Vancouver answered in the third period, scoring the game's deciding goal, and then, when Medicine Hat pulled its goalie in desperation, Vancouver scored a third time.

In the aftermath of the game, the players and their families and sports reporters from across the country crammed into the winning team's locker room. The air was filled with cigar smoke and the smell of champagne and sweat-soaked hockey gear. On the wall was a hand-painted banner: "Embrace the Struggle." In the center of the room the Giants' coach, Don Hay, stood misty-eyed. "I'm just so proud of these guys," he said. "Just look around the locker room. There isn't one guy who didn't buy in wholeheartedly."

Canadian hockey is a meritocracy. Thousands of Canadian boys begin to play the sport at the "novice" level, before they are even in kindergarten. From that point on, there are leagues for every age class, and at each of those levels, the players are sifted and sorted and evaluated, with the most talented separated out and groomed for the next level. By the time players reach their midteens, the very best of the best have been channeled into an elite league known as Major Junior A, which is the top of the pyramid. And if your Major Junior A team plays for the Memorial Cup, that means you are at the very top of the top of the pyramid.

This is the way most sports pick their future stars. It's the way soccer is organized in Europe and South America, and it's the way Olympic athletes are chosen. For that matter, it is not all that different from the way the world of classical music picks its future virtuosos, or the way the world of ballet picks its future ballerinas, or the way our elite educational system picks its future scientists and intellectuals.

You can't buy your way into Major Junior A hockey. It doesn't matter who your father or mother is, or who your grandfather was, or what business your family is in. Nor does it matter if you live in the most remote corner of the most northerly province in Canada. If you have ability, the vast network of hockey scouts and talent spotters will find you, and if you are willing to work to develop that ability, the system will reward you. Success in hockey is based on *individual merit*—and both of those words are important. Players are judged on their own performance, not on anyone else's, and on the basis of their ability, not on some other arbitrary fact.

Or are they?

2.

This is a book about outliers, about men and women who do things that are out of the ordinary. Over the course of the chapters ahead, I'm going to introduce you to one kind of outlier after another: to geniuses, business tycoons, rock stars, and software programmers. We're going to uncover the secrets of a remarkable lawyer, look at what separates the very best pilots from pilots who have crashed planes, and try to figure out why Asians are so good at math. And in examining the lives of the remarkable among us—the skilled, the talented, and the driven— I will argue that there is something profoundly wrong with the way we make sense of success.

What is the question we always ask about the successful? We want to know what they're *like*—what kind of personalities they have, or how intelligent they are, or what kind of lifestyles they have, or what special talents they might have been born with. And we assume that it is those personal qualities that explain how that individual reached the top.

In the autobiographies published every year by the billionaire/entrepreneur/rock star/celebrity, the story line is always the same: our hero is born in modest circumstances and by virtue of his own grit and talent fights his way to greatness. In the Bible, Joseph is cast out by his brothers and sold into slavery and then rises to become the pharaoh's right-hand man on the strength of his own brilliance and insight. In the famous nineteenth-century novels of Horatio Alger, young boys born into poverty rise to riches through a combination of pluck and initiative. "I think overall it's a disadvantage," Jeb Bush once said of what it meant for his business career that he was the son of an American president and the brother of an American president and the grandson of a wealthy Wall Street banker and US senator. When he ran for governor of Florida, he repeatedly referred to himself as a "self-made man," and it is a measure of how deeply we associate success with the efforts of the individual that few batted an eye at that description.

"Lift up your heads," Robert Winthrop told the crowd many years ago at the unveiling of a statue of that great hero of American independence Benjamin Franklin, "and look at the image of a man who rose from nothing, who owed nothing to parentage or patronage, who enjoyed no advantages of early education which are not open—a hundredfold open—to yourselves, who performed the most menial services in the businesses in which his early life was employed, but who lived to stand before Kings, and died to leave a name which the world will never forget."

In *Outliers*, I want to convince you that these kinds of personal explanations of success don't work. People don't rise from nothing. We do owe something to parentage and patronage. The people who stand before kings may look like they did it all by themselves. But in fact they are invariably the beneficiaries of hidden advantages and extraordinary opportunities and cultural legacies that allow them to learn and work hard and make sense of the world in ways others cannot. It makes a difference where and when we grew up. The culture we belong to and the legacies passed down by our forebears shape the patterns of our achievement in ways we cannot begin to imagine. It's not enough to ask what successful people are like, in other words. It is only by asking where they are *from* that we can unravel the logic behind who succeeds and who doesn't.

Biologists often talk about the "ecology" of an organism: the tallest oak in the forest is the tallest not just because it grew from the hardiest acorn; it is the tallest also because no other trees blocked its sunlight, the soil around it was deep and rich, no rabbit chewed through its bark as a sapling, and no lumberjack cut it down before it matured. We all know that successful people come from hardy seeds. But do we know enough about the sunlight that warmed them, the soil in which they put down the roots, and the rabbits and lumberjacks they were lucky enough to avoid? This is not a book about tall trees. It's a book about forests—and hockey is a good place to start because the explanation for who gets to the top of the hockey world is a lot more interesting and complicated than it looks. In fact, it's downright peculiar.

3.

Here is the player roster of the 2007 Medicine Hat Tigers. Take a close look and see if you can spot anything strange about it.

No.	Name	Pos.	L/R	Height	Weight	Birth Date	Hometown
9	Brennan Bosch	C	R	5'8"	173	Feb. 14, 1988	Martensville, SK
11	Scott Wasden	C	R	6'1"	188	Jan. 4, 1988	Westbank, BC
12	Colton Grant	LW	L	5'9"	177	Mar. 20, 1989	Standard, AB
14	Darren Helm	LW	L	6'	182	Jan. 21, 1987	St. Andrews, MB
15	Derek Dorsett	RW	L	5'11"	178	Dec. 20, 1986	Kindersley, SK
16	Daine Todd	C	R	5'10"	173	Jan. 10, 1987	Red Deer, AB
17	Tyler Swystun	RW	R	5'11"	185	Jan. 15, 1988	Cochrane, AB
19	Matt Lowry	C	R	6'	186	Mar. 2, 1988	Neepawa, MB
20	Kevin Undershute	LW	L	6'	178	Apr. 12, 1987	Medicine Hat, AB
21	Jerrid Sauer	RW	R	5'10"	196	Sep. 12, 1987	Medicine Hat, AB
22	Tyler Ennis	C	L	5'9"	160	Oct. 6, 1989	Edmonton, AB
23	Jordan Hickmott	C	R	6'	183	Apr. 11, 1990	Mission, BC

25	Jakub Rumpel	RW	R	5'8"	166	Jan. 27, 1987	Hrnciarovce, SLO
28	Bretton Cameron	C	R	5'11"	168	Jan. 26, 1989	Didsbury, AB
36	Chris Stevens	LW	L	5'10"	197	Aug. 20, 1986	Dawson Creek, BC
3	Gord Baldwin	D	L	6'5"	205	Mar. 1, 1987	Winnipeg, MB
4	David Schlemko	D	L	6'1"	195	May 7, 1987	Edmonton, AB
5	Trever Glass	D	L	6'	190	Jan. 22, 1988	Cochrane, AB
10	Kris Russell	D	L	5'10"	177	May 2, 1987	Caroline, AB
18	Michael Sauer	D	R	6'3"	205	Aug. 7, 1987	Sartell, MN
24	Mark Isherwood	D	R	6'	183	Jan. 31, 1989	Abbotsford, BC
27	Shayne Brown	D	L	6'1"	198	Feb. 20, 1989	Stony Plain, AB
29	Jordan Bendfeld	D	R	6'3"	230	Feb. 9, 1988	Leduc, AB
31	Ryan Holfeld	G	L	5'11"	166	Jun. 29, 1989	LeRoy, SK
33	Matt Keetley	G	R	6'2"	189	Apr. 27, 1986	Medicine Hat, AB

Do you see it? Don't feel bad if you don't, because for many years in the hockey world no one did. It wasn't until the mid-1980s, in fact, that a Canadian psychologist named Roger Barnsley first drew attention to the phenomenon of relative age.

Barnsley was at a Lethbridge Broncos hockey game in southern Alberta, a team that played in the same Major Junior A league as the Vancouver Giants and the Medicine Hat Tigers. He was there with his wife, Paula, and their two boys, and his wife was reading the program, when she ran across a roster list just like the one above that you just looked at.

"Roger," she said, "do you know when these young men were born?"

Barnsley said yes. "They're all between sixteen and twenty, so they'd be born in the late sixties."

"No, no," Paula went on. "What *month*."

"I thought she was crazy," Barnsley remembers. "But I looked through it, and what she was saying just jumped out at me. For some reason, there were an incredible number of January, February, and March birth dates."

Barnsley went home that night and looked up the birth dates of as many professional hockey players as he could find. He saw the same pattern. Barnsley, his wife, and a colleague, A. H. Thompson, then gathered statistics on every player in the Ontario Junior Hockey League. The story was the same. More players were born in January than in any other month, and by an overwhelming margin. The second most frequent birth month? February. The third? March. Barnsley found that there were nearly five and a half times as many Ontario Junior Hockey League players born in January as were born in November. He looked at the all-star teams of eleven-year-olds and thirteen-year-olds—the young players selected for elite traveling squads. Same story. He looked at the composition of the National Hockey League. Same story. The more he looked, the more Barnsley came to believe that what he was seeing was not a chance occurrence but an iron law of Canadian hockey: in *any* elite group of hockey players—the very best of the best—40 percent of the players will have been born between January and March, 30 percent between April and June, 20 percent between July and September, and 10 percent between October and December.

"In all my years in psychology, I have never run into an effect this large," Barnsley says. "You don't even need to do any statistical analysis. You just look at it."

Look back at the Medicine Hat roster. Do you see it now? Seventeen out of the twenty-five players on the team were born in January, February, March, or April.

Here is the play-by-play for the first two goals in the Memorial Cup final, only this time I've substituted the players' birthdays for their names. It no longer sounds like the championship of Canadian junior hockey. It now sounds like a strange sporting ritual for teenage boys born under the astrological signs Capricorn, Aquarius, and Pisces.

March 11 starts around one side of the Tigers' net, leaving the puck for his teammate January 4, who passes it to January 22, who flips it back to March 12, who shoots point-blank at the Tigers' goalie, April 27. April 27 blocks the shot, but it's rebounded by Vancouver's March 6. He shoots! Medicine Hat defensemen February 9 and February 14 dive to block the puck while January 10 looks on helplessly. March 6 scores!

Let's go to the second period now.

Medicine Hat's turn. The Tigers' scoring leader, January 21, charges down the right side of the ice. He stops and circles, eluding the Vancouver defenseman February 15. January 21 then deftly passes the puck to his teammate December 20—wow! what's he doing out there?!—who shrugs off the onrushing defender May 17 and slides a cross-crease pass back to January 21. He shoots! Vancouver defenseman March 12 dives, trying to block the shot. Vancouver's goalie, March 19, lunges helplessly. January 21 scores! He raises his hands in triumph. His teammate May 2 jumps on his back with joy.

4.

The explanation for this is quite simple. It has nothing to do with astrology, nor is there anything magical about the first three months of the year. It's simply that in Canada the eligibility cutoff for age-class hockey is January 1. A boy who turns ten on January 2, then, could be playing alongside someone who doesn't turn ten until the end of the year—and at that age, in preadolescence, a twelve-month gap in age represents an enormous difference in physical maturity.

This being Canada, the most hockey-crazed country on earth, coaches start to select players for the traveling "rep" squad—the all-star teams—at the age of nine or ten, and of course they are more likely to view as talented the bigger and more coordinated players, who have had the benefit of critical extra months of maturity.

And what happens when a player gets chosen for a rep squad? He gets better coaching, and his teammates are better, and he plays fifty or seventy-five games a season instead of twenty games a season like those left behind in the "house" league, and he practices twice as much as, or even three times more than, he would have otherwise. In the beginning, his advantage isn't so much that he is inherently better but only that he is a little older. But by the age of thirteen or fourteen, with the benefit of better coaching and all that extra practice under his belt, he really *is* better, so he's the one more likely to make it to the Major Junior A league, and from there into the big leagues.[*]

Barnsley argues that these kinds of skewed age distributions exist whenever three things happen: selection, streaming, and differentiated experience. If you make a decision about who is good and who is not good at an early age; if you separate the "talented" from the "untalented"; and if you provide the "talented" with a superior experience, then you're going to end up giving a huge advantage to that small group of people born closest to the cutoff date.

In the United States, football and basketball don't select, stream, and differentiate quite as dramatically. As a result, a child can be a bit behind physically in those sports and still play as much as his or her more mature peers.[*] But baseball does. The cutoff date for almost all nonschool baseball leagues in the United States is July 31, with the result that more major league players are born in August than in any other month. (The numbers are striking:

in 2005, among Americans playing major league baseball 505 were born in August versus 313 born in July.)

European soccer, similarly, is organized like hockey and baseball—and the birth-date distributions in that sport are heavily skewed as well. In England, the eligibility date is September 1, and in the football association's premier league at one point in the 1990s, there were 288 players born between September and November and only 136 players born between June and August. In international soccer, the cutoff date used to be August 1, and in one recent junior world championship tournament, 135 players were born in the three months after August 1, and just 22 were born in May, June, and July. Today the cutoff date for international junior soccer is January 1. Take a look at the roster of the 2007 Czech National Junior soccer team, which made the Junior World Cup finals.

Here we go again:

No.	Player	Birth Date	Position
1	Marcel Gecov	Jan. 1, 1988	MF
2	Ludek Frydrych	Jan. 3, 1987	GK
3	Petr Janda	Jan. 5, 1987	MF
4	Jakub Dohnalek	Jan. 12, 1988	DF
5	Jakub Mares	Jan. 26, 1987	MF
6	Michal Held	Jan. 27, 1987	DF
7	Marek Strestik	Feb. 1, 1987	FW
8	Jiri Valenta	Feb. 14, 1988	MF
9	Jan Simunek	Feb. 20, 1987	DF
10	Tomas Oklestek	Feb. 21, 1987	MF
11	Lubos Kalouda	Feb. 21, 1987	MF
12	Radek Petr	Feb. 24, 1987	GK
13	Ondrej Mazuch	Mar. 15, 1989	DF
14	Ondrej Kudela	Mar. 26, 1987	MF
15	Marek Suchy	Mar. 29, 1988	DF
16	Martin Fenin	Apr. 16, 1987	FW
17	Tomas Pekhart	May 26, 1989	FW
18	Lukas Kuban	Jun. 22, 1987	DF
19	Tomas Cihlar	Jun. 24, 1987	DF
20	Tomas Frystak	Aug. 18, 1987	GK
21	Tomas Micola	Sep. 26, 1988	MF

At the national team tryouts, the Czech soccer coaches might as well have told everyone born after midsummer that they should pack their bags and go home.

Hockey and soccer are just games, of course, involving a select few. But these exact same biases also show up in areas of much more consequence, like education. Parents with a child born at the end of the calendar year often think about holding their child back before the start of kindergarten: it's hard for a five-year-old to keep up with a child born many months earlier. But most parents, one suspects, think that whatever disadvantage a younger child faces in kindergarten eventually goes away. *But it doesn't.* It's just like hockey. The small initial advantage that the child born in the early part of the year has over the child born at the end of the year persists. It locks children into patterns of achievement and underachievement, encouragement and discouragement, that stretch on and on for years.

Recently, two economists—Kelly Bedard and Elizabeth Dhuey—looked at the relationship between scores on what is called the Trends in International Mathematics and Science Study, or TIMSS (math and science tests given every four years to children in many countries around the world), and month of birth. They found that among fourth graders, the oldest children scored somewhere between four and twelve percentile points better than the youngest children. That, as Dhuey explains, is a "huge effect." It means that if you take two intellectually equivalent fourth graders with birthdays at opposite ends of the cutoff date, the older student could score in the eightieth percentile, while the younger one could score in the sixty-eighth percentile. That's the difference between qualifying for a gifted program and not.

"It's just like sports," Dhuey said. "We do ability grouping early on in childhood. We have advanced reading groups and advanced math groups. So, early on, if we look at young kids, in kindergarten and first grade, the teachers are confusing maturity with ability. And they put the older kids in the advanced stream, where they learn better skills; and the next year, because they are in the higher groups, they do even better; and the next year, the same thing happens, and they do even better again. The only country we don't see this going on is Denmark. They have a national policy where they have no ability grouping until the age of ten." Denmark waits to make selection decisions until maturity differences by age have evened out.

Dhuey and Bedard subsequently did the same analysis, only this time looking at college. What did they find? At four-year colleges in the United States—the highest stream of postsecondary education—students belonging to the relatively youngest group in their class are underrepresented by about 11.6 percent. That initial difference in maturity doesn't go away with time. It persists. And for thousands of students, that initial disadvantage is the difference between going to college—and having a real shot at the middle class—and not.[*]

"I mean, it's ridiculous," Dhuey says. "It's outlandish that our arbitrary choice of cutoff dates is causing these long-lasting effects, and no one seems to care about them."

5.

Think for a moment about what the story of hockey and early birthdays says about success.

It tells us that our notion that it is the best and the brightest who effortlessly rise to the top is much too simplistic. Yes, the hockey players who make it to the professional level are more talented than you or me. But they also got a big head start, an opportunity that they neither deserved nor earned. And that opportunity played a critical role in their success.

The sociologist Robert Merton famously called this phenomenon the "Matthew Effect" after the New Testament verse in the Gospel of Matthew: "For unto everyone that hath shall be given, and he shall have abundance. But from him that hath not shall be taken away even that which he hath." It is those who are successful, in other words, who are most likely to be given the kinds of special opportunities that lead to further success. It's the rich who get the biggest tax breaks. It's the best students who get the best teaching and most attention. And it's the biggest nine- and ten-year-olds who get the most coaching and practice. Success is the result of what sociologists like to call "accumulative advantage." The professional hockey player starts out a little bit better than his peers. And that little difference leads to an opportunity that makes that difference a bit bigger, and that edge in turn leads to another opportunity, which makes the initially small difference bigger still—and on and on until the hockey player is a genuine outlier. But he didn't start out an outlier. He started out just a little bit better.

The second implication of the hockey example is that the systems we set up to determine who gets ahead aren't particularly efficient. We think that starting all-star leagues and gifted programs as early as possible is the best way of ensuring that no talent slips through the cracks. But take a look again at that roster for the Czech Republic soccer team. There are no players born in July, October, November, or December, and only one each in August and September. Those born in the last half of the year have all been discouraged, or overlooked, or pushed out of the sport. *The talent of essentially half of the Czech athletic population has been squandered.*

So what do you do if you're an athletic young Czech with the misfortune to have been born in the last part of the year? You *can't* play soccer. The deck is stacked against you. So maybe you could play the other sport that Czechs are obsessed with—hockey. But wait. (I think you know what's coming.) Here's the roster of the 2007 Czech junior hockey team that finished fifth at the world championships.

No.	Player	Birth Date	Position
1	David Kveton	Jan. 3, 1988	Forward
2	Jiri Suchy	Jan. 3, 1988	Defense
3	Michael Kolarz	Jan. 12, 1987	Defense
4	Jakub Vojta	Feb. 8, 1987	Defense
5	Jakub Kindl	Feb. 10, 1987	Defense
6	Michael Frolik	Feb. 17, 1989	Forward
7	Martin Hanzal	Feb. 20, 1987	Forward
8	Tomas Svoboda	Feb. 24, 1987	Forward
9	Jakub Cerny	Mar. 5, 1987	Forward
10	Tomas Kudelka	Mar. 10, 1987	Defense
11	Jaroslav Barton	Mar. 26, 1987	Defense
12	H. O. Pozivil	Apr. 22, 1987	Defense
13	Daniel Rakos	May 25, 1987	Forward
14	David Kuchejda	Jun. 12, 1987	Forward
15	Vladimir Sobotka	Jul. 2, 1987	Forward
16	Jakub Kovar	Jul. 19, 1988	Goalie
17	Lukas Vantuch	Jul. 20, 1987	Forward
18	Jakub Voracek	Aug. 15, 1989	Forward
19	Tomas Pospisil	Aug. 25, 1987	Forward
20	Ondrej Pavelec	Aug. 31, 1987	Goalie
21	Tomas Kana	Nov. 29, 1987	Forward
22	Michal Repik	Dec. 31, 1988	Forward

Those born in the last quarter of the year might as well give up on hockey too.

Do you see the consequences of the way we have chosen to think about success? Because we so profoundly personalize success, we miss opportunities to lift others onto the top rung. We make rules that frustrate achievement. We prematurely write off people as failures. We are too much in awe of those who succeed and far too dismissive of those who fail. And, most of all, we become much too passive. We overlook just how large a role we all play—and by "we" I mean society—in determining who makes it and who doesn't.

If we chose to, we could acknowledge that cutoff dates matter. We could set up two or even three hockey leagues, divided up by month of birth. Let the players develop on separate tracks and then pick all-star teams. If all the Czech and Canadian athletes born at the end of the year had a fair chance, then the Czech and the Canadian national teams suddenly would have twice as many athletes to choose from.

Schools could do the same thing. Elementary and middle schools could put the January through April–born students in one class, the May through August in another class, and those born in September through December in the third class. They could let students learn with and compete against other students of the same maturity level. It would be a little bit more complicated administratively. But it wouldn't necessarily cost that much more money, and it would level the playing field for those who—through no fault of their own—have been dealt a big disadvantage by the educational system. We could easily take control of the machinery of achievement, in other words—not just in sports but, as we will see, in other more consequential areas as well. But we don't. And why? Because we cling to the idea that success is a simple function of individual merit and that the world in which we all grow up and the rules we choose to write as a society don't matter at all.

6.

Before the Memorial Cup final, Gord Wasden—the father of one of the Medicine Hat Tigers—stood by the side of the ice, talking about his son Scott. He was wearing a Medicine Hat baseball cap and a black Medicine Hat T-shirt. "When he was four and five years old," Wasden remembered, "his little brother was in a walker, and he would shove a hockey stick in his hand and they would play hockey on the floor in the kitchen, morning till night. Scott *always* had a passion for it. He played rep hockey throughout his minor-league hockey career. He always made the Triple A teams. As a first-year peewee or a first-year bantam, he always played on the [top] rep team." Wasden was clearly nervous: his son was about to play in the biggest game of his life. "He's had to work very hard for whatever he's got. I'm very proud of him."

Those were the ingredients of success at the highest level: passion, talent, and hard work. But there was another element. When did Wasden first get the sense that his son was something special? "You know, he was always a bigger kid for his age. He was strong, and he had a knack for scoring goals at an early age. And he was always kind of a standout for his age, a captain of his team…."

Bigger kid for his age? Of course he was. Scott Wasden was born on January 4, within three days of the absolute perfect birthday for an elite hockey player. He was one of the lucky ones. If the eligibility date for Canadian hockey were later in the year, he might have been watching the Memorial Cup championship from the stands instead of playing on the ice.

CHAPTER TWO

The 10,000-Hour Rule

"IN HAMBURG, WE HAD TO PLAY FOR EIGHT HOURS."

1.

The University of Michigan opened its new Computer Center in 1971, in a brand-new building on Beal Avenue in Ann Arbor, with beige-brick exterior walls and a dark-glass front. The university's enormous mainframe computers stood in the middle of a vast white room, looking, as one faculty member remembers, "like one of the last scenes in the movie *2001: A Space Odyssey.*" Off to the side were dozens of keypunch machines—what passed in those days for computer terminals. In 1971, this was state of the art. The University of Michigan had one of the most advanced computer science programs in the world, and over the course of the Computer Center's life, thousands of students passed through that white room, the most famous of whom was a gawky teenager named Bill Joy.

Joy came to the University of Michigan the year the Computer Center opened. He was sixteen. He was tall and very thin, with a mop of unruly hair. He had been voted "Most Studious Student" by his graduating class at North Farmington High School, outside Detroit, which, as he puts it, meant that he was a "no-date nerd." He had thought he might end up as biologist or a mathematician. But late in his freshman year, he stumbled across the Computer Center—and he was hooked.

From that point on, the Computer Center was his life. He programmed whenever he could. Joy got a job with a computer science professor so he could program over the summer. In 1975, he enrolled in graduate school at the University of California at Berkeley. There, he buried himself even deeper in the world of computer software. During the oral exams for his PhD, he made up a particularly complicated algorithm on the fly that, as one of his many admirers has written, "so stunned his examiners [that] one of them later compared the experience to 'Jesus confounding his elders.' "

Working in collaboration with a small group of programmers, Joy took on the task of rewriting UNIX, which was a software system developed by AT&T for mainframe computers. Joy's version was very good. It was so good, in fact, that it became—and remains—the operating system on which literally millions of computers around the world run. "If you put your Mac in that funny mode where you can see the code," Joy says, "I see things that I remember typing in twenty-five years ago." And do you know who wrote much of the software that allows you to access the Internet? Bill Joy.

After graduating from Berkeley, Joy cofounded the Silicon Valley firm Sun Microsystems, which was one of the most critical players in the computer revolution. There he rewrote another computer language—Java—and his legend grew still further. Among Silicon Valley insiders, Joy is spoken of with as much awe as someone like Bill Gates of Microsoft. He is sometimes called the Edison of the Internet. As the Yale computer scientist David Gelernter says, "Bill Joy is one of the most influential people in the modern history of computing."

The story of Bill Joy's genius has been told many times, and the lesson is always the same. Here was a world that was the purest of meritocracies. Computer programming didn't operate as an old-boy network, where you got ahead because of money or connections. It was a wide-open field in which all participants were judged solely on their talent and their accomplishments. It was a world where the best men won, and Joy was clearly one of those best men.

It would be easier to accept that version of events, however, if we hadn't just looked at hockey and soccer players. Theirs was supposed to be a pure meritocracy as well. Only it wasn't. It was a story of how the outliers in a particular field reached their lofty status through a combination of ability, opportunity, and utterly arbitrary advantage.

Is it possible the same pattern of special opportunities operate in the real world as well? Let's go back over the story of Bill Joy and find out.

2.

For almost a generation, psychologists around the world have been engaged in a spirited debate over a question that most of us would consider to have been settled years ago. The question is this: is there such a thing as innate talent? The obvious answer is yes. Not every hockey player born in January ends up playing at the professional level. Only some do—the innately talented ones. Achievement is talent plus preparation. The problem with this view is that the closer psychologists look at the careers of the gifted, the smaller the role innate talent seems to play and the bigger the role preparation seems to play.

Exhibit A in the talent argument is a study done in the early 1990s by the psychologist K. Anders Ericsson and two colleagues at Berlin's elite Academy of Music. With the help of the Academy's professors, they divided the school's violinists into three groups. In the first group were the stars, the students with the potential to become world-class soloists. In the second were those judged to be merely "good." In the third were students who were unlikely to ever play professionally and who intended to be music teachers in the public school system. All of the violinists were then asked the same question: over the course of your entire career, ever since you first picked up the violin, how many hours have you practiced?

Everyone from all three groups started playing at roughly the same age, around five years old. In those first few years, everyone practiced roughly the same amount, about two or three hours a week. But when the students were around the age of eight, real differences started to emerge. The students who would end up the best in their class began to practice more than everyone else: six hours a week by age nine, eight hours a week by age twelve, sixteen hours a week by age fourteen, and up and up, until by the age of twenty they were practicing—that is, purposefully and single-mindedly playing their instruments with the intent to get better—well over thirty hours a week. In fact, by the age of twenty, the elite performers had each totaled ten thousand hours of practice. By contrast, the merely good students had totaled eight thousand hours, and the future music teachers had totaled just over four thousand hours.

Ericsson and his colleagues then compared amateur pianists with professional pianists. The same pattern emerged. The amateurs never practiced more than about three hours a week over the course of their childhood, and by the age of twenty they had totaled two thousand hours of practice. The professionals, on the other hand, steadily increased their practice time every year, until by the age of twenty they, like the violinists, had reached ten thousand hours.

The striking thing about Ericsson's study is that he and his colleagues couldn't find any "naturals," musicians who floated effortlessly to the top while practicing a fraction of the time their peers did. Nor could they find any "grinds," people who worked harder than everyone else, yet just didn't have what it takes to break the top ranks. Their research suggests that once a musician has enough ability to get into a top music school, the thing that distinguishes one performer from another is how hard he or she works. That's it. And what's more, the people at the very top don't work just harder or even much harder than everyone else. They work much, *much* harder.

The idea that excellence at performing a complex task requires a critical minimum level of practice surfaces again and again in studies of expertise. In fact, researchers have settled on what they believe is the magic number for true expertise: ten thousand hours.

"The emerging picture from such studies is that ten thousand hours of practice is required to achieve the level of mastery associated with being a world-class expert—in anything," writes the neurologist Daniel Levitin. "In study after study, of composers, basketball players, fiction writers, ice skaters, concert pianists, chess players, master criminals, and what have you, this number comes up again and again. Of course, this doesn't address why some people get more out of their practice sessions than others do. But no one has yet found a case in which true world-class expertise was accomplished in less time. It seems that it takes the brain this long to assimilate all that it needs to know to achieve true mastery."

This is true even of people we think of as prodigies. Mozart, for example, famously started writing music at six. But, writes the psychologist Michael Howe in his book *Genius Explained,*

by the standards of mature composers, Mozart's early works are not outstanding. The earliest pieces were all probably written down by his father, and perhaps improved in the process. Many of Wolfgang's childhood compositions, such as the first seven of his concertos for piano and orchestra, are largely arrangements of works by other composers. Of those concertos that only contain music original to Mozart, the earliest that is now regarded as a masterwork (No. 9, K. 271) was not composed until he was twenty-one: by that time Mozart had already been composing concertos for ten years.

The music critic Harold Schonberg goes further: Mozart, he argues, actually "developed late," since he didn't produce his greatest work until he had been composing for more than twenty years.

To become a chess grandmaster also seems to take about ten years. (Only the legendary Bobby Fischer got to that elite level in less than that amount of time: it took him nine years.) And what's ten years? Well, it's roughly how long it takes to put in ten thousand hours of hard practice. Ten thousand hours is the magic number of greatness.

Here is the explanation for what was so puzzling about the rosters of the Czech and Canadian national sports teams. There was practically no one on those teams born after September 1, which doesn't seem to make any sense. You'd think that there should be a fair number of Czech hockey or soccer prodigies born late in the year who are *so* talented that they eventually make their way into the top tier as young adults, despite their birth dates.

But to Ericsson and those who argue against the primacy of talent, that isn't surprising at all. That late-born prodigy doesn't get chosen for the all-star team as an eight-year-old because he's too small. So he doesn't get the extra practice. And without that extra practice, he has no chance at hitting ten thousand hours by the time the professional hockey teams start looking for players. And without ten thousand hours under his belt, there is no way he can ever master the skills necessary to play at the top level. Even Mozart—the greatest musical prodigy of all time—couldn't hit his stride until he had his ten thousand hours in. Practice isn't the thing you do once you're good. It's the thing you do that makes you good.

The other interesting thing about that ten thousand hours, of course, is that ten thousand hours is an *enormous* amount of time. It's all but impossible to reach that number all by yourself by the time you're a young adult. You have to have parents who encourage and support you. You can't be poor, because if you have to hold down a part-time job on the side to help make ends meet, there won't be time left in the day to practice enough. In fact, most people can reach that number only if they get into some kind of special program—like a hockey all-star squad—or if they get some kind of extraordinary opportunity that gives them a chance to put in those hours.

3.

So, back to Bill Joy. It's 1971. He's tall and gawky and sixteen years old. He's the math whiz, the kind of student that schools like MIT and Caltech and the University of Waterloo attract by the hundreds. "When Bill was a little kid, he wanted to know everything about everything way before he should've even known he wanted to know," his father, William, says. "We answered him when we could. And when we couldn't, we would just give him a book." When it came time to apply to college, Joy got a perfect score on the math portion of the Scholastic Aptitude Test. "It wasn't particularly hard," he says matter-of-factly. "There was plenty of time to check it twice."

He has talent by the truckload. But that's not the only consideration. It never is. The key to his development is that he stumbled across that nondescript building on Beal Avenue.

In the early 1970s, when Joy was learning about programming, computers were the size of rooms. A single machine (which might have less power and memory than your microwave now has) could cost upwards of a million dollars —and that's in 1970s dollars. Computers were rare. If you found one, it was hard to get access to it; if you managed to get access, renting time on it cost a fortune.

What's more, programming itself was extraordinarily tedious. This was the era when computer programs were created using cardboard punch cards. Each line of code was imprinted on the card using a keypunch machine. A complex program might include hundreds, if not thousands, of these cards in tall stacks. Once a program was ready, you walked over to whatever mainframe computer you had access to and gave the stack of cards to an operator. Since computers could handle only one task at a time, the operator made an appointment for your program, and depending on how many people were ahead of you in line, you might not get your cards back for a few hours or even a day. And if you made even a single error—even a typographical error—in your program, you had to take the cards back, track down the error, and begin the whole process again.

Under those circumstances, it was exceedingly difficult for anyone to become a programming expert. Certainly becoming an expert by your early twenties was all but impossible. When you can "program" for only a few minutes out of every hour you spend in the computer room, how can you ever get in ten thousand hours of practice? "Programming with cards," one computer scientist from that era remembers, "did not teach you programming. It taught you patience and proofreading."

It wasn't until the mid-1960s that a solution to the programming problem emerged. Computers were finally powerful enough that they could handle more than one "appointment" at once. If the computer's operating system was rewritten, computer scientists realized, the machine's time could be shared; the computer could be trained to handle hundreds of tasks at the same time. That, in turn, meant that programmers didn't have to physically hand their stacks of computer cards to the operator anymore. Dozens of terminals could be built, all linked to the mainframe by a telephone line, and everyone could be working—online—all at once.

Here is how one history of the period describes the advent of time-sharing:

> This was not just a revolution. It was a revelation. Forget the operator, the card decks, the wait. With time-sharing, you could sit at your Teletype, bang in a couple of commands, and get an answer then and there. Time-sharing was interactive: A program could ask for a response, wait for you to type it in, act on it while you waited, and show you the result, all in "real time."

This is where Michigan came in, because Michigan was one of the first universities in the world to switch over to time-sharing. By 1967, a prototype of the system was up and running. By the early 1970s, Michigan had enough computing power that a hundred people could be programming simultaneously in the Computer Center. "In the late sixties, early seventies, I don't think there was anyplace else that was exactly like Michigan," Mike Alexander, one of the pioneers of Michigan's computing system, said. "Maybe MIT. Maybe Carnegie Mellon. Maybe Dartmouth. I don't think there were any others."

This was the opportunity that greeted Bill Joy when he arrived on the Ann Arbor campus in the fall of 1971. He hadn't chosen Michigan because of its computers. He had never done anything with computers in high school. He was interested in math and engineering. But when the programming bug hit him in his freshman year, he found himself—by the happiest of accidents—in one of the few places in the world where a seventeen-year-old could program all he wanted.

"Do you know what the difference is between the computing cards and time-sharing?" Joy says. "It's the difference between playing chess by mail and speed chess." Programming wasn't an exercise in frustration anymore. It was *fun.*

"I lived in the north campus, and the Computer Center was in the north campus," Joy went on. "How much time did I spend there? Oh, a phenomenal amount of time. It was open twenty-four hours. I would stay there all night, and just walk home in the morning. In an average week in those years, I was spending more time in the Computer Center than on my classes. All of us down there had this recurring nightmare of forgetting to show up for class at all, of not even realizing we were enrolled.

"The challenge was that they gave all the students an account with a fixed amount of money, so your time would run out. When you signed on, you would put in how long you wanted to spend on the computer. They gave you, like, an hour of time. That's all you'd get. But someone figured out that if you put in 'time equals' and then a letter, like t equals k, they wouldn't charge you," he said, laughing at the memory. "It was a bug in the software. You could put in t equals k and sit there forever."

Just look at the stream of opportunities that came Bill Joy's way. Because he happened to go to a farsighted school like the University of Michigan, he was able to practice on a time-sharing system instead of with punch cards; because the Michigan system happened to have a bug in it, he could program all he wanted; because the university was willing to spend the money to keep the Computer Center open twenty-four hours, he could stay up all night; and because he was able to put in so many hours, by the time he happened to be presented with the opportunity to rewrite UNIX, he was up to the task. Bill Joy was brilliant. He wanted to learn. That was a big part of it. But before he could become an expert, someone had to give him the opportunity to learn *how* to be an expert.

"At Michigan, I was probably programming eight or ten hours a day," he went on. "By the time I was at Berkeley I was doing it day and night. I had a terminal at home. I'd stay up until two or three o'clock in the morning, watching old movies and programming. Sometimes I'd fall asleep at the keyboard"—he mimed his head falling on the keyboard—"and you know how the key repeats until the end, and it starts to go beep, beep, beep? After that happens three times, you have to go to bed. I was still relatively incompetent even when I got to Berkeley. I was proficient by my second year there. That's when I wrote programs that are still in use today, thirty years later." He paused for a moment to do the math in his head—which for someone like Bill Joy doesn't take very long. Michigan in 1971. Programming in earnest by sophomore year. Add in the summers, then the days and nights in his first year at Berkeley. "So, so maybe… ten thousand hours?" he said, finally. "That's about right."

4.

Is the ten-thousand-hour rule a general rule of success? If we scratch below the surface of every great achiever, do we always find the equivalent of the Michigan Computer Center or the hockey all-star team—some sort of special opportunity for practice?

Let's test the idea with two examples, and for the sake of simplicity, let's make them as familiar as possible: the Beatles, one of the most famous rock bands ever; and Bill Gates, one of the world's richest men.

The Beatles—John Lennon, Paul McCartney, George Harrison, and Ringo Starr—came to the United States in February of 1964, starting the so-called British Invasion of the American music scene and putting out a string of hit records that transformed the face of popular music.

The first interesting thing about the Beatles for our purposes is how long they had already been together by the time they reached the United States. Lennon and McCartney first started playing together in 1957, seven years prior to landing in America. (Incidentally, the time that elapsed between their founding and their arguably greatest artistic achievements—*Sgt. Pepper's Lonely Hearts Club Band* and *The Beatles* [White Album]—is ten years.) And if you look even more closely at those long years of preparation, you'll find an experience that, in the context of hockey players and Bill Joy and world-class violinists, sounds awfully familiar. In 1960, while they were still just a struggling high school rock band, they were invited to play in Hamburg, Germany.

"Hamburg in those days did not have rock-and-roll music clubs. It had strip clubs," says Philip Norman, who wrote the Beatles biography *Shout!* "There was one particular club owner called Bruno, who was originally a fairground showman. He had the idea of bringing in rock groups to play in various clubs. They had this formula. It was a huge nonstop show, hour after hour, with a lot of people lurching in and the other lot lurching out. And the bands would play all the time to catch the passing traffic. In an American red-light district, they would call it nonstop striptease.

"Many of the bands that played in Hamburg were from Liverpool," Norman went on. "It was an accident. Bruno went to London to look for bands. But he happened to meet an entrepreneur from Liverpool in Soho who was down in London by pure chance. And he arranged to send some bands over. That's how the connection was established. And eventually the Beatles made a connection not just with Bruno but with other club owners as well. They kept going back because they got a lot of alcohol and a lot of sex."

And what was so special about Hamburg? It wasn't that it paid well. It didn't. Or that the acoustics were fantastic. They weren't. Or that the audiences were savvy and appreciative. They were anything but. It was the sheer amount of time the band was forced to play.

Here is John Lennon, in an interview after the Beatles disbanded, talking about the band's performances at a Hamburg strip club called the Indra:

We got better and got more confidence. We couldn't help it with all the experience playing all night long. It was handy them being foreign. We had to try even harder, put our heart and soul into it, to get ourselves over.

In Liverpool, we'd only ever done one-hour sessions, and we just used to do our best numbers, the same ones, at every one. In Hamburg, we had to play for eight hours, so we really had to find a new way of playing.

Eight hours?

Here is Pete Best, the Beatles' drummer at the time: "Once the news got out about that we were making a show, the club started packing them in. We played seven nights a week. At first we played almost nonstop till twelve-thirty, when it closed, but as we got better the crowds stayed till two most mornings."

Seven days a week?

The Beatles ended up traveling to Hamburg five times between 1960 and the end of 1962. On the first trip, they played 106 nights, five or more hours a night. On their second trip, they played 92 times. On their third trip, they played 48 times, for a total of 172 hours on stage. The last two Hamburg gigs, in November and December of 1962, involved another 90 hours of performing. All told, they performed for 270 nights in just over a year and a half. By the time they had their first burst of success in 1964, in fact, they had performed live an estimated twelve hundred times. Do you know how extraordinary that is? Most bands today don't perform twelve hundred times in their entire careers. The Hamburg crucible is one of the things that set the Beatles apart.

"They were no good onstage when they went there and they were very good when they came back," Norman went on. "They learned not only stamina. They had to learn an enormous amount of numbers—cover versions of everything you can think of, not just rock and roll, a bit of jazz too. They weren't disciplined onstage at all before that. But when they came back, they sounded like no one else. It was the making of them."

5.

Let's now turn to the history of Bill Gates. His story is almost as well known as the Beatles'. Brilliant, young math whiz discovers computer programming. Drops out of Harvard. Starts a little computer company called Microsoft with his friends. Through sheer brilliance and ambition and guts builds it into the giant of the software world. That's the broad outline. Let's dig a little bit deeper.

Gates's father was a wealthy lawyer in Seattle, and his mother was the daughter of a well-to-do banker. As a child Bill was precocious and easily bored by his studies. So his parents took him out of public school and, at the beginning of seventh grade, sent him to Lakeside, a private school that catered to Seattle's elite families. Midway through Gates's second year at Lakeside, the school started a computer club.

"The Mothers' Club at school did a rummage sale every year, and there was always the question of what the money would go to," Gates remembers. "Some went to the summer program, where inner-city kids would come up to the campus. Some of it would go for teachers. That year, they put three thousand dollars into a computer terminal down in this funny little room that we subsequently took control of. It was kind of an amazing thing."

It was an "amazing thing," of course, because this was 1968. Most *colleges* didn't have computer clubs in the 1960s. Even more remarkable was the kind of computer Lakeside bought. The school didn't have its students learn programming by the laborious computer-card system, like virtually everyone else was doing in the 1960s. Instead, Lakeside installed what was called an ASR-33 Teletype, which was a time-sharing terminal with a direct link to a mainframe computer in downtown Seattle. "The whole idea of time-sharing only got invented in nineteen sixty-five," Gates continued. "Someone was pretty forward-looking." Bill Joy got an extraordinary, early opportunity to learn programming on a time-share system as a freshman in college, in 1971. Bill Gates got to do real-time programming *as an eighth grader in 1968.*

From that moment forward, Gates lived in the computer room. He and a number of others began to teach themselves how to use this strange new device. Buying time on the mainframe computer the ASR was hooked up to was, of course, expensive—even for a wealthy institution like Lakeside—and it wasn't long before the $3,000 put up by the Mothers' Club ran out. The parents raised more money. The students spent it. Then a group of programmers at the University of Washington formed an outfit called Computer Center Corporation (or C-Cubed), which leased computer time to local companies. As luck would have it, one of the founders of the firm—Monique Rona—had a son at Lakeside, a year ahead of Gates. Would the Lakeside computer club, Rona wondered, like to test out the company's software programs on the weekends in exchange for free programming time? Absolutely! After school, Gates took the bus to the C-Cubed offices and programmed long into the evening.

C-Cubed eventually went bankrupt, so Gates and his friends began hanging around the computer center at the University of Washington. Before long, they latched onto an outfit called ISI (Information Sciences Inc.), which agreed to let them have free computer time in exchange for working on a piece of software that could be used to automate company payrolls. In one seven-month period in 1971, Gates and his cohorts ran up 1,575 hours of computer time on the ISI mainframe, which averages out to eight hours a day, seven days a week.

"It was my obsession," Gates says of his early high school years. "I skipped athletics. I went up there at night. We were programming on weekends. It would be a rare week that we wouldn't get twenty or thirty hours in. There was a period where Paul Allen and I got in trouble for stealing a bunch of passwords and crashing the system. We got kicked out. I didn't get to use the computer the whole summer. This is when I was fifteen and sixteen. Then I found out Paul had found a computer that was free at the University of Washington. They had these machines in the medical center and the physics department. They were on a twenty-four-hour schedule, but with this big slack period, so that between three and six in the morning they never scheduled anything." Gates laughed. "I'd leave at night, after my bedtime. I could walk up to the University of Washington from my house. Or I'd take the bus. That's why I'm always so generous to the University of Washington, because they let me steal so much computer time." (Years later, Gates's mother said, "We always wondered why it was so hard for him to get up in the morning.")

One of the founders of ISI, Bud Pembroke, then got a call from the technology company TRW, which had just signed a contract to set up a computer system at the huge Bonneville Power station in southern Washington State. TRW desperately needed programmers familiar with the particular software the power station used. In these early days of the computer revolution, programmers with that kind of specialized experience were hard to find. But Pembroke knew exactly whom to call: those high school kids from Lakeside who had been running up thousands of hours of computer time on the ISI mainframe. Gates was now in his senior year, and somehow he managed to convince his teachers to let him decamp for Bonneville under the guise of an independent study project. There he spent the spring writing code, supervised by a man named John Norton, who Gates says taught him as much about programming as almost anyone he'd ever met.

Those five years, from eighth grade through the end of high school, were Bill Gates's Hamburg, and by any measure, he was presented with an even more extraordinary series of opportunities than Bill Joy.

Opportunity number one was that Gates got sent to Lakeside. How many high schools in the world had access to a time-sharing terminal in 1968? Opportunity number two was that the mothers of Lakeside had enough money to pay for the school's computer fees. Number three was that, when that money ran out, one of the parents happened to work at C-Cubed, which happened to need someone to check its code on the weekends, and which also happened not to care if weekends turned into weeknights. Number four was that Gates just happened to find out about ISI, and ISI just happened to need someone to work on its payroll software. Number five was that Gates happened to live within walking distance of the University of Washington. Number six was that the university happened to have free computer time between three and six in the morning. Number seven was that TRW happened to call Bud Pembroke. Number eight was that the best programmers Pembroke knew for that particular problem happened to be two high school kids. And number nine was that Lakeside was willing to let those kids spend their spring term miles away, writing code.

And what did virtually all of those opportunities have in common? They gave Bill Gates extra time to practice. By the time Gates dropped out of Harvard after his sophomore year to try his hand at his own software company, he'd been programming practically nonstop for seven consecutive years. He was *way* past ten thousand hours. How many teenagers in the world had the kind of experience Gates had? "If there were fifty in the world, I'd be stunned," he says. "There was C-Cubed and the payroll stuff we did, then TRW—all those things came together. I had a better exposure to software development at a young age than I think anyone did in that period of time, and all because of an incredibly lucky series of events."

If we put the stories of hockey players and the Beatles and Bill Joy and Bill Gates together, I think we get a more complete picture of the path to success. Joy and Gates and the Beatles are all undeniably talented. Lennon and McCartney had a musical gift of the sort that comes along once in a generation, and Bill Joy, let us not forget, had a mind so quick that he was able to make up a complicated algorithm on the fly that left his professors in awe. That much is obvious.

But what truly distinguishes their histories is not their extraordinary talent but their extraordinary opportunities. The Beatles, for the most random of reasons, got invited to go to Hamburg. Without Hamburg, the Beatles might well have taken a different path. "I was very lucky," Bill Gates said at the beginning of our interview. That doesn't mean he isn't brilliant or an extraordinary entrepreneur. It just means that he understands what incredible good fortune it was to be at Lakeside in 1968.

All the outliers we've looked at so far were the beneficiaries of some kind of unusual opportunity. Lucky breaks don't seem like the exception with software billionaires and rock bands and star athletes. They seem like the rule.

Let me give you one final example of the hidden opportunities that outliers benefit from. Suppose we do another version of the calendar analysis we did in the previous chapter with hockey players, only this time looking at birth years, not birth months. To start with, take a close look at the following list of the seventy-five richest people in human history. The net worth of each person is calculated in current US dollars. As you can see, it includes queens and kings and pharaohs from centuries past, as well as contemporary billionaires, such as Warren Buffett and Carlos Slim.

No.	Name	Wealth in Billions (USD)	Origin	Company or Source of Wealth
1	John D. Rockefeller	318.3	United States	Standard Oil
2	Andrew Carnegie	298.3	Scotland	Carnegie Steel Company
3	Nicholas II of Russia	253.5	Russia	House of Romanov
4	William Henry Vanderbilt	231.6	United States	Chicago, Burlington and Quincy Railroad
5	Osman Ali Khan, Asaf Jah VII	210.8	Hyderabad	Monarchy
			United	

Rank	Name	Wealth	Country	Source
6	Andrew W. Mellon	188.8	United States	Gulf Oil
7	Henry Ford	188.1	United States	Ford Motor Company
8	Marcus Licinius Crassus	169.8	Roman Republic	Roman Senate
9	Basil II	169.4	Byzantine Empire	Monarchy
10	Cornelius Vanderbilt	167.4	United States	New York and Harlem Railroad
11	Alanus Rufus	166.9	England	Investments
12	Amenophis III	155.2	Ancient Egypt	Pharaoh
13	William de Warenne, 1st Earl of Surrey	153.6	England	Earl of Surrey
14	William II of England	151.7	England	Monarchy
15	Elizabeth I	142.9	England	House of Tudor
16	John D. Rockefeller Jr.	141.4	United States	Standard Oil
17	Sam Walton	128.0	United States	Wal-Mart
18	John Jacob Astor	115.0	Germany	American Fur Company
19	Odo of Bayeux	110.2	England	Monarchy
20	Stephen Girard	99.5	France	First Bank of the United States
21	Cleopatra	95.8	Ancient Egypt	Ptolemaic Inheritance
22	Stephen Van Rensselaer III	88.8	United States	Rensselaerswyck Estate
23	Richard B. Mellon	86.3	United States	Gulf Oil
24	Alexander Turney Stewart	84.7	Ireland	Long Island Rail Road
25	William Backhouse Astor Jr.	84.7	United States	Inheritance
26	Don Simon Iturbi Patiño	81.2	Bolivia	Huanuni tin mine
27	Sultan Hassanal Bolkiah	80.7	Brunei	Kral
28	Frederick Weyerhaeuser	80.4	Germany	Weyerhaeuser Corporation
29	Moses Taylor	79.3	United States	Citibank
30	Vincent Astor	73.9	United States	Inheritance
31	Carlos Slim Helú	72.4	Mexico	Telmex
32	T. V. Soong	67.8	China	Central Bank of China

33	Jay Gould	67.1	United States	Union Pacific
34	Marshall Field	66.3	United States	Marshall Field and Company
35	George F. Baker	63.6	United States	Central Railroad of New Jersey
36	Hetty Green	58.8	United States	Seaboard National Bank
37	Bill Gates	58.0	United States	Microsoft
38	Lawrence Joseph Ellison	58.0	United States	Oracle Corporation
39	Richard Arkwright	56.2	England	Derwent Valley Mills
40	Mukesh Ambani	55.8	India	Reliance Industries
41	Warren Buffett	52.4	United States	Berkshire Hathaway
42	Lakshmi Mittal	51.0	India	Mittal Steel Company
43	J. Paul Getty	50.1	United States	Getty Oil Company
44	James G. Fair	47.2	United States	Consolidated Virginia Mining Company
45	William Weightman	46.1	United States	Merck & Company
46	Russell Sage	45.1	United States	Western Union
47	John Blair	45.1	United States	Union Pacific
48	Anil Ambani	45.0	India	Reliance Communications
49	Leland Stanford	44.9	United States	Central Pacific Railroad
50	Howard Hughes Jr.	43.4	United States	Hughes Tool Company, Hughes Aircraft Company, Summa Corporation, TWA
51	Cyrus Curtis	43.2	United States	Curtis Publishing Company
52	John Insley Blair	42.4	United States	Delaware, Lackawanna and Western Railroad
53	Edward Henry Harriman	40.9	United States	Union Pacific Railroad
54	Henry H. Rogers	40.9	United States	Standard Oil Company
55	Paul Allen	40.0	United States	Microsoft, Vulcan Inc.
56	John Kluge	40.0	Germany	Metropolitan Broadcasting Company
57	J. P. Morgan	39.8	United States	General Electric, US Steel
58	Oliver H. Payne	38.8	United States	Standard Oil Company
59	Yoshiaki Tsutsumi	38.1	Japan	Seibu Corporation

No.	Name	Wealth	Country	Source
60	Henry Clay Frick	37.7	United States	Carnegie Steel Company
61	John Jacob Astor IV	37.0	United States	Inheritance
62	George Pullman	35.6	United States	Pullman Company
63	Collis Potter Huntington	34.6	United States	Central Pacific Railroad
64	Peter Arrell Brown Widener	33.4	United States	American Tobacco Company
65	Philip Danforth Armour	33.4	United States	Armour Refrigerator Line
66	William S. O'Brien	33.3	United States	Consolidated Virginia Mining Company
67	Ingvar Kamprad	33.0	Sweden	IKEA
68	K. P. Singh	32.9	India	DLF Universal Limited
69	James C. Flood	32.5	United States	Consolidated Virginia Mining Company
70	Li Ka-shing	32.0	China	Hutchison Whampoa Limited
71	Anthony N. Brady	31.7	United States	Brooklyn Rapid Transit
72	Elias Hasket Derby	31.4	United States	Shipping
73	Mark Hopkins	30.9	United States	Central Pacific Railroad
74	Edward Clark	30.2	United States	Singer Sewing Machine
75	Prince Al-Waleed bin Talal	29.5	Saudi Arabia	Kingdom Holding Company

Do you know what's interesting about that list? Of the seventy-five names, an astonishing fourteen are Americans born within nine years of one another in the mid-nineteenth century. Think about that for a moment. Historians start with Cleopatra and the pharaohs and comb through every year in human history ever since, looking in every corner of the world for evidence of extraordinary wealth, and almost 20 percent of the names they end up with come from a single generation in a single country.

Here's the list of those Americans and their birth years:

   1. John D. Rockefeller, 1839
   2. Andrew Carnegie, 1835
 28. Frederick Weyerhaeuser, 1834
 33. Jay Gould, 1836

34. Marshall Field, 1834

35. George F. Baker, 1840

36. Hetty Green, 1834

44. James G. Fair, 1831

54. Henry H. Rogers, 1840

57. J. P. Morgan, 1837

58. Oliver H. Payne, 1839

62. George Pullman, 1831

64. Peter Arrell Brown Widener, 1834

65. Philip Danforth Armour, 1832

What's going on here? The answer becomes obvious if you think about it. In the 1860s and 1870s, the American economy went through perhaps the greatest transformation in its history. This was when the railroads were being built and when Wall Street emerged. It was when industrial manufacturing started in earnest. It was when all the rules by which the traditional economy had functioned were broken and remade. What this list says is that it really matters how old you were when that transformation happened.

If you were born in the late 1840s you missed it. You were too young to take advantage of that moment. If you were born in the 1820s you were too old: your mind-set was shaped by the pre–Civil War paradigm. But there was a particular, narrow nine-year window that was just perfect for seeing the potential that the future held. All of the fourteen men and women on the list above had vision and talent. But they also were given an extraordinary opportunity, in the same way that hockey and soccer players born in January, February, and March are given an extraordinary opportunity.*

Now let's do the same kind of analysis for people like Bill Joy and Bill Gates.

If you talk to veterans of Silicon Valley, they'll tell you that the most important date in the history of the personal computer revolution was January 1975. That was when the magazine *Popular Electronics* ran a cover story on an extraordinary machine called the Altair 8800. The Altair cost $397. It was a do-it-yourself contraption that you could assemble at home. The headline on the story read: "PROJECT BREAKTHROUGH! World's First Minicomputer Kit to Rival Commercial Models."

To the readers of *Popular Electronics,* in those days the bible of the fledgling software and computer world, that headline was a revelation. Computers up to that point had been the massive, expensive mainframes of the sort sitting in the white expanse of the Michigan Computer Center. For years, every hacker and electronics whiz had dreamt of the day when a computer would come along that was small and inexpensive enough for an ordinary person to use and own. That day had finally arrived.

If January 1975 was the dawn of the personal computer age, then who would be in the best position to take advantage of it? The same principles apply here that applied to the era of John Rockefeller and Andrew Carnegie.

"If you're too old in nineteen seventy-five, then you'd already have a job at IBM out of college, and once people started at IBM, they had a real hard time making the transition to the new world," says Nathan Myhrvold, who was a top executive at Microsoft for many years. "You had this multibillion-dollar company making mainframes, and if you were part of that, you'd think, Why screw around with these little pathetic computers? That was the computer industry to those people, and it had nothing to do with this new revolution. They were blinded by that being the only vision of computing. They made a nice living. It's just that there was no opportunity to become a zillionaire and make an impact on the world."

If you were more than a few years out of college in 1975, then you belonged to the old paradigm. You had just bought a house. You're married. A baby is on the way. You're in no position to give up a good job and pension for some pie-in-the-sky $397 computer kit. So let's rule out all those born before, say, 1952.

At the same time, though, you don't want to be too young. You really want to get in on the ground floor, right in 1975, and you can't do that if you're still in high school. So let's also rule out anyone born after, say, 1958. The perfect age to be in 1975, in other words, is old enough to be a part of the coming revolution but not so old that you missed it. Ideally, you want to be twenty or twenty-one, which is to say, born in 1954 or 1955.

There is an easy way to test this theory. When was Bill Gates born?

Bill Gates: October 28, 1955

That's the perfect birth date! Gates is the hockey player born on January 1. Gates's best friend at Lakeside was Paul Allen. He also hung out in the computer room with Gates and shared those long evenings at ISI and C-Cubed. Allen went on to found Microsoft with Bill Gates. When was Paul Allen born?

Paul Allen: January 21, 1953

The third-richest man at Microsoft is the one who has been running the company on a day-to-day basis since 2000, one of the most respected executives in the software world, Steve Ballmer. Ballmer's birth date?

Steve Ballmer: March 24, 1956

Let's not forget a man every bit as famous as Gates: Steve Jobs, the cofounder of Apple Computer. Unlike Gates, Jobs wasn't from a rich family and he didn't go to Michigan, like Joy. But it doesn't take much investigation of his upbringing to realize that he had his Hamburg too. He grew up in Mountain View, California, just south of San Francisco, which is the absolute epicenter of Silicon Valley. His neighborhood was filled with engineers from Hewlett-Packard, then as now one of the most important electronics firms in the world. As a teenager he prowled the flea markets of Mountain View, where electronics hobbyists and tinkerers sold spare parts. Jobs came of age breathing the air of the very business he would later dominate.

This paragraph from *Accidental Millionaire,* one of the many Jobs biographies, gives us a sense of how extraordinary his childhood experiences were. Jobs

    attended evening talks by Hewlett-Packard scientists. The talks were
    about the latest advances in electronics and Jobs, exercising a style that
    was a trademark of his personality, collared Hewlett-Packard engineers
    and drew additional information from them. Once he even called Bill
    Hewlett, one of the company's founders, to request parts. Jobs not only
    received the parts he asked for, he managed to wrangle a summer job.
    Jobs worked on an assembly line to build computers and was so
    fascinated that he tried to design his own...

Wait. *Bill Hewlett gave him spare parts?* That's on a par with Bill Gates getting unlimited access to a time-share terminal at age thirteen. It's as if you were interested in fashion and your neighbor when you were growing up happened to be Giorgio Armani. And when was Jobs born?

Steve Jobs: February 24, 1955

Another of the pioneers of the software revolution was Eric Schmidt. He ran Novell, one of Silicon Valley's most important software firms, and in 2001, he became the chief executive officer of Google. Birth date?

Eric Schmidt: April 27, 1955

I don't mean to suggest, of course, that every software tycoon in Silicon Valley was born in 1955. Some weren't, just as not every business titan in the United States was born in the mid-1830s. But there are very clearly patterns here, and what's striking is how little we seem to want to acknowledge them. We pretend that success is exclusively a matter of individual merit. But there's nothing in any of the histories we've looked at so far to suggest things are that simple. These are stories, instead, about people who were given a special opportunity to work really hard and seized it, and who happened to come of age at a time when that extraordinary effort was rewarded by the rest of society. Their success was not just of their own making. It was a product of the world in which they grew up.

By the way, let's not forget Bill Joy. Had he been just a little bit older and had he had to face the drudgery of programming with computer cards, he says, he would have studied science. Bill Joy the computer legend would have been Bill Joy the biologist. And had he come along a few years later, the little window that gave him the chance to write the supporting code for the Internet would have closed. Again, Bill Joy the computer legend might well have been Bill Joy the biologist. When was Bill Joy born?

Bill Joy: November 8, 1954

Joy would go on, after his stint at Berkeley, to become one of the four founders of Sun Microsystems, one of the oldest and most important of Silicon Valley's software companies. And if you still think that accidents of time and place and birth don't matter all that much, here are the birthdays of the three other founders of Sun Microsystems:

Scott McNealy: November 13, 1954
Vinod Khosla: January 28, 1955
Andy Bechtolsheim: September 30, 1955

CHAPTER THREE

The Trouble with Geniuses, Part 1

"KNOWLEDGE OF A BOY'S IQ IS OF LITTLE HELP IF YOU ARE FACED WITH A FORMFUL OF CLEVER BOYS."

1.

In the fifth episode of the 2008 season, the American television quiz show *1 vs. 100* had as its special guest a man named Christopher Langan.

The television show *1 vs. 100* is one of many that sprang up in the wake of the phenomenal success of *Who Wants to Be a Millionaire*. It features a permanent gallery of one hundred ordinary people who serve as what is called the "mob." Each week they match wits with a special invited guest. At stake is a million dollars. The guest has to be smart enough to answer more questions correctly than his or her one hundred adversaries—and by that standard, few have ever seemed as superbly qualified as Christopher Langan.

"Tonight the mob takes on their fiercest competition yet," the voice-over began. "Meet Chris Langan, who many call the smartest man in America." The camera did a slow pan of a stocky, muscular man in his fifties. "The average person has an IQ of one hundred," the voice-over continued. "Einstein one fifty. Chris has an IQ of one ninety-five. He's currently wrapping his big brain around a theory of the universe. But will his king-size cranium be enough to take down the mob for one million dollars? Find out right now on *One versus One Hundred*."

Out strode Langan onto the stage amid wild applause.

"You don't think you need to have a high intellect to do well on *One versus One Hundred*, do you?" the show's host, Bob Saget, asked him. Saget looked at Langan oddly, as if he were some kind of laboratory specimen.

"Actually, I think it could be a hindrance," Langan replied. He had a deep, certain voice. "To have a high IQ, you tend to specialize, think deep thoughts. You avoid trivia. But now that I see these people"—he glanced at the mob, the amusement in his eyes betraying just how ridiculous he found the proceedings —"I think I'll do okay."

Over the past decade, Chris Langan has achieved a strange kind of fame. He has become the public face of genius in American life, a celebrity outlier. He gets invited on news shows and profiled in magazines, and he has been the subject of a documentary by the filmmaker Errol Morris, all because of a brain that appears to defy description.

The television news show *20/20* once hired a neuropsychologist to give Langan an IQ test, and Langan's score was literally off the charts—too high to be accurately measured. Another time, Langan took an IQ test specially designed for people too smart for ordinary IQ tests. He got all the questions right except one.[*] He was speaking at six months of age. When he was three, he would listen to the radio on Sundays as the announcer read the comics aloud, and he would follow along on his own until he had taught himself to read. At five, he began questioning his grandfather about the existence of God—and remembers being disappointed in the answers he got.

In school, Langan could walk into a test in a foreign-language class, not having studied at all, and if there were two or three minutes before the instructor arrived, he could skim through the textbook and ace the test. In his early teenage years, while working as a farmhand, he started to read widely in the area of theoretical physics. At sixteen, he made his way through Bertrand Russell and Alfred North Whitehead's famously abstruse masterpiece *Principia Mathematica*. He got a perfect score on his SAT, even though he fell asleep at one point during the test.

"He did math for an hour," his brother Mark says of Langan's summer routine in high school. "Then he did French for an hour. Then he studied Russian. Then he would read philosophy. He did that religiously, every day."

Another of his brothers, Jeff, says, "You know, when Christopher was fourteen or fifteen, he would draw things just as a joke, and it would be like a photograph. When he was fifteen, he could match Jimi Hendrix lick for lick on a guitar. Boom. Boom. Boom. Half the time, Christopher didn't attend school at all. He would just show up for tests and there was nothing they could do about it. To us, it was hilarious. He could brief a semester's worth of textbooks in two days, and take care of whatever he had to take care of, and then get back to whatever he was doing in the first place."[*]

On the set of *1 vs. 100*, Langan was poised and confident. His voice was deep. His eyes were small and fiercely bright. He did not circle about topics, searching for the right phrase, or double back to restate a previous sentence. For that matter, he did not say um, or ah, or use any form of conversational mitigation: his sentences came marching out, one after another, polished and crisp, like soldiers on a parade ground. Every question Saget threw at him, he tossed aside, as if it were a triviality. When his winnings reached $250,000, he appeared to make a mental calculation that the risks of losing everything were at that point greater than the potential benefits of staying in. Abruptly, he stopped. "I'll take the cash," he said. He shook Saget's hand firmly and was finished— exiting on top as, we like to think, geniuses invariably do.

2.

Just after the First World War, Lewis Terman, a young professor of psychology at Stanford University, met a remarkable boy named Henry Cowell. Cowell had been raised in poverty and chaos. Because he did not get along with other children, he had been unschooled since the age of seven. He worked as a janitor at a one-room schoolhouse not far from the Stanford campus, and throughout the day, Cowell would sneak away from his job and play the school piano. And the music he made was beautiful.

Terman's specialty was intelligence testing; the standard IQ test that millions of people around the world would take during the following fifty years, the Stanford-Binet, was his creation. So he decided to test Cowell's IQ. The boy *must* be intelligent, he reasoned, and sure enough, he was. He had an IQ of above 140, which is near genius level. Terman was fascinated. How many other diamonds in the rough were there? he wondered.

He began to look for others. He found a girl who knew the alphabet at nineteen months, and another who was reading Dickens and Shakespeare by the time she was four. He found a young man who had been kicked out of law school because his professors did not believe that it was possible for a human being to precisely reproduce long passages of legal opinions from memory.

In 1921, Terman decided to make the study of the gifted his life work. Armed with a large grant from the Commonwealth Foundation, he put together a team of fieldworkers and sent them out into California's elementary schools. Teachers were asked to nominate the brightest students in their classes. Those children were given an intelligence test. The students who scored in the top 10 percent were then given a second IQ test, and those who scored above 130 on that test were given a third IQ test, and from that set of results Terman selected the best and the brightest. By the time Terman was finished, he had sorted through the records of some 250,000 elementary and high school students, and identified 1,470 children whose IQs averaged over 140 and ranged as high as 200. That group of young geniuses came to be known as the "Termites," and they were the subjects of what would become one of the most famous psychological studies in history.

For the rest of his life, Terman watched over his charges like a mother hen. They were tracked and tested, measured and analyzed. Their educational attainments were noted, marriages followed, illnesses tabulated, psychological health charted, and every promotion and job change dutifully recorded. Terman wrote his recruits letters of recommen-dation for jobs and graduate school applications. He doled out a constant stream of advice and counsel, all the time recording his findings in thick red volumes entitled *Genetic Studies of Genius.*

"There is nothing about an individual as important as his IQ, except possibly his morals," Terman once said. And it was to those with a very high IQ, he believed, that "we must look for production of leaders who advance science, art, government, education and social welfare generally." As his subjects grew older, Terman issued updates on their progress, chronicling their extraordinary achievements. "It is almost impossible," Terman wrote giddily, when his charges were in high school, "to read a newspaper account of any sort of competition or activity in which California boys and girls participate without finding among the winners the names of one or more… members of our gifted group." He took writing samples from some of his most artistically minded subjects and had literary critics compare them to the early writings of famous authors. They could find no difference. All the signs pointed, he said, to a group with the potential for "heroic stature." Terman believed that his Termites were destined to be the future elite of the United States.

Today, many of Terman's ideas remain central to the way we think about success. Schools have programs for the "gifted." Elite universities often require that students take an intelligence test (such as the American Scholastic Aptitude Test) for admission. High-tech companies like Google or Microsoft carefully measure the cognitive abilities of prospective employees out of the same belief: they are convinced that those at the very top of the IQ scale have the greatest potential. (At Microsoft, famously, job applicants are asked a battery of questions designed to test their smarts, including the classic "Why are manhole covers round?" If you don't know the answer to that question, you're not smart enough to work at Microsoft.[*])

If I had magical powers and offered to raise your IQ by 30 points, you'd say yes—right? You'd assume that would help you get further ahead in the world. And when we hear about someone like Chris Langan, our instinctive response is the same as Terman's instinctive response when he met Henry Cowell almost a century ago. We feel awe. Geniuses are the ultimate outliers. Surely there is nothing that can hold someone like that back.

But is that true?

So far in *Outliers,* we've seen that extraordinary achievement is less about talent than it is about opportunity. In this chapter, I want to try to dig deeper into why that's the case by looking at the outlier in its purest and most distilled form —the genius. For years, we've taken our cues from people like Terman when it comes to understanding the significance of high intelligence. But, as we shall see, Terman made an error. He was wrong about his Termites, and had he happened on the young Chris Langan working his way through *Principia Mathematica* at the age of sixteen, he would have been wrong about him for the same reason. Terman didn't understand what a real outlier was, and that's a mistake we continue to make to this day.

3.

One of the most widely used intelligence tests is something called Raven's Progressive Matrices. It requires no language skills or specific body of acquired knowledge. It's a measure of abstract reasoning skills. A typical Raven's test consists of forty-eight items, each one harder than the one before it, and IQ is calculated based on how many items are answered correctly.

Here's a question, typical of the sort that is asked on the Raven's.

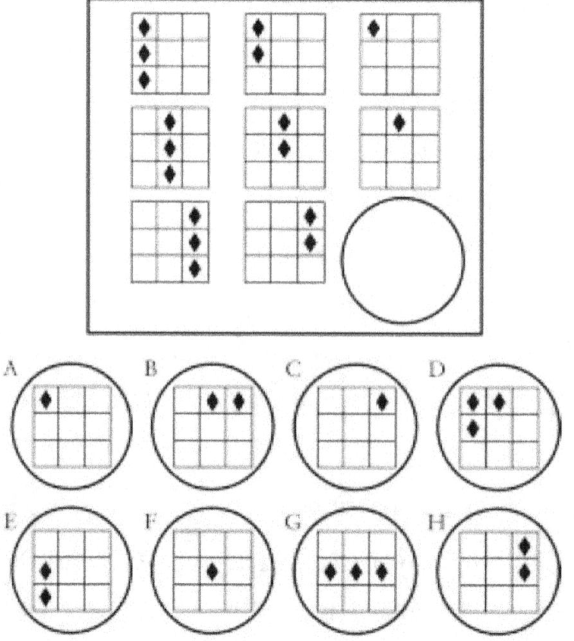

Did you get that? I'm guessing most of you did. The correct answer is C. But now try this one. It's the kind of really hard question that comes at the end of the Raven's.

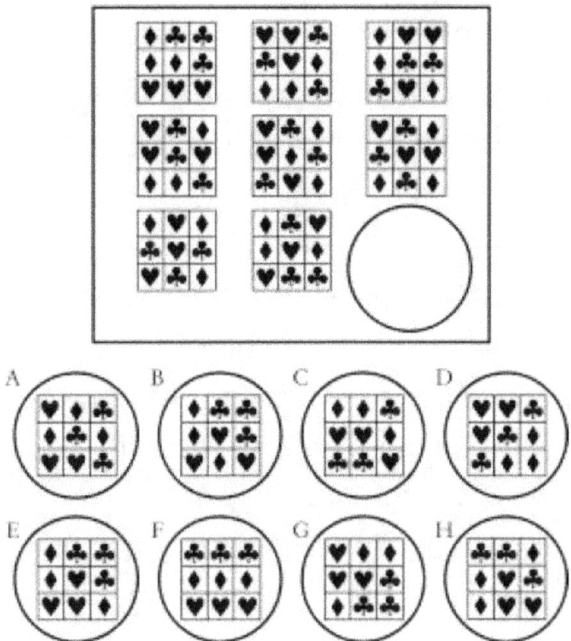

The correct answer is A. I have to confess I couldn't figure this one out, and I'm guessing most of you couldn't either. Chris Langan almost certainly could, however. When we say that people like Langan are really brilliant, what we mean is that they have the kind of mind that can figure out puzzles like that last question.

Over the years, an enormous amount of research has been done in an attempt to determine how a person's performance on an IQ test like the Raven's translates to real-life success. People at the bottom of the scale—with an IQ below 70—are considered mentally disabled. A score of 100 is average; you probably need to be just above that mark to be able to handle college. To get into and succeed in a reasonably competitive graduate program, meanwhile, you probably need an IQ of at least 115. In general, the higher your score, the more education you'll get, the more money you're likely to make, and—believe it or not—the longer you'll live.

But there's a catch. The relationship between success and IQ works only up to a point. Once someone has reached an IQ of somewhere around 120, having additional IQ points doesn't seem to translate into any measurable real-world advantage.[*]

"It is amply proved that someone with an IQ of 170 is more likely to think well than someone whose IQ is 70," the British psychologist Liam Hudson has written, "and this holds true where the comparison is much closer—between IQs of, say, 100 and 130. But the relation seems to break down when one is making comparisons between two people both of whom have IQs which are relatively high…. A mature scientist with an adult IQ of 130 is as likely to win a Nobel Prize as is one whose IQ is 180."

What Hudson is saying is that IQ is a lot like height in basketball. Does someone who is five foot six have a realistic chance of playing professional basketball? Not really. You need to be at least six foot or six one to play at that level, and, all things being equal, it's probably better to be six two than six one, and better to be six three than six two. But past a certain point, height stops mattering so much. A player who is six foot eight is not automatically better than someone two inches shorter. (Michael Jordan, the greatest player ever, was six six after all.) A basketball player only has to be tall *enough*—and the same is true of intelligence. Intelligence has a threshold.

The introduction to the *1 vs. 100* episode pointed out that Einstein had an IQ of 150 and Langan has an IQ of 195. Langan's IQ is 30 percent higher than Einstein's. But that doesn't mean Langan is 30 percent *smarter* than Einstein. That's ridiculous. All we can say is that when it comes to thinking about really hard things like physics, they are both clearly smart *enough*.

The idea that IQ has a threshold, I realize, goes against our intuition. We think that, say, Nobel Prize winners in science must have the highest IQ scores imaginable; that they must be the kinds of people who got perfect scores on their entrance examinations to college, won every scholarship available, and had such stellar academic records in high school that they were scooped up by the top universities in the country.

But take a look at the following list of where the last twenty-five Americans to win the Nobel Prize in Medicine got their undergraduate degrees, starting in 2007.

Antioch College
Brown University
UC Berkeley
University of Washington
Columbia University
Case Institute of Technology
MIT

Caltech
Harvard University
Hamilton College
Columbia University
University of North Carolina
DePauw University
University of Pennsylvania
University of Minnesota
University of Notre Dame
Johns Hopkins University
Yale University
Union College, Kentucky
University of Illinois
University of Texas
Holy Cross
Amherst College
Gettysburg College
Hunter College

No one would say that this list represents the college choices of the absolute best high school students in America. Yale and Columbia and MIT are on the list, but so are DePauw, Holy Cross, and Gettysburg College. It's a list of *good* schools.

Along the same lines, here are the colleges of the last twenty-five American Nobel laureates in Chemistry:

City College of New York
City College of New York
Stanford University
University of Dayton, Ohio
Rollins College, Florida
MIT
Grinnell College
MIT
McGill University

Georgia Institute of Technology
Ohio Wesleyan University
Rice University
Hope College
Brigham Young University
University of Toronto
University of Nebraska
Dartmouth College
Harvard University
Berea College
Augsburg College
University of Massachusetts
Washington State University
University of Florida
University of California, Riverside
Harvard University

To be a Nobel Prize winner, apparently, you have to be smart enough to get into a college at least as good as Notre Dame or the University of Illinois. That's all.[*]

This is a radical idea, isn't it? Suppose that your teenage daughter found out that she had been accepted at two universities—Harvard University and Georgetown University, in Washington, DC. Where would you want her to go? I'm guessing Harvard, because Harvard is a "better" school. Its students score a good 10 to 15 percent higher on their entrance exams.

But given what we are learning about intelligence, the idea that schools can be ranked, like runners in a race, makes no sense. Georgetown's students may not be as smart on an absolute scale as the students of Harvard. But they are all, clearly, smart enough, and future Nobel Prize winners come from schools like Georgetown as well as from schools like Harvard.

The psychologist Barry Schwartz recently proposed that elite schools give up their complex admissions process and simply hold a lottery for everyone above the threshold. "Put people into two categories," Schwartz says. "Good enough and not good enough. The ones who are good enough get put into a hat. And those who are not good enough get rejected." Schwartz concedes that his idea has virtually no chance of being accepted. But he's absolutely right. As Hudson writes (and keep in mind that he did his research at elite all-male English boarding schools in the 1950s and 1960s), "Knowledge of a boy's IQ is of little help *if you are faced with a formful of clever boys.*"[*]

Let me give you an example of the threshold effect in action. The University of Michigan law school, like many elite US educational institutions, uses a policy of affirmative action when it comes to applicants from disadvantaged backgrounds. Around 10 percent of the students Michigan enrolls each fall are members of racial minorities, and if the law school did not significantly relax its entry requirements for those students—admitting them with lower undergraduate grades and lower standardized-test scores than everyone else—it estimates that percentage would be less than 3 percent. Furthermore, if we compare the grades that the minority and nonminority students get in law school, we see that the white students do better. That's not surprising: if one group has higher undergraduate grades and test scores than the other, it's almost certainly going to have higher grades in law school as well. This is one reason that affirmative action programs are so controversial. In fact, an attack on the University of Michigan's affirmative action program recently went all the way to the US Supreme Court. For many people it is troubling that an elite educational institution lets in students who are less qualified than their peers.

A few years ago, however, the University of Michigan decided to look closely at how the law school's minority students had fared after they graduated. How much money did they make? How far up in the profession did they go? How satisfied were they with their careers? What kind of social and community contributions did they make? What kind of honors had they won? They looked at everything that could conceivably be an indication of real-world success. And what they found surprised them.

"We knew that our minority students, a lot of them, were doing well," says Richard Lempert, one of the authors of the Michigan study. "I think our expectation was that we would find a half- or two-thirds-full glass, that they had not done as well as the white students but nonetheless a lot were quite successful. But we were completely surprised. We found that they were doing every bit as well. There was no place we saw any serious discrepancy."

What Lempert is saying is that by the only measure that a law school really ought to care about—how well its graduates do in the real world—minority students aren't less qualified. They're just as successful as white students. And why? Because even though the academic credentials of minority students at Michigan aren't as good as those of white students, the quality of students at the law school is high enough that *they're still above the threshold*. They are smart enough. Knowledge of a law student's test scores is of little help if you are faced with a classroom of clever law students.

4.

Let's take the threshold idea one step further. If intelligence matters only up to a point, then past that point, other things—things that have nothing to do with intelligence—must start to matter more. It's like basketball again: once someone is tall enough, then we start to care about speed and court sense and agility and ball-handling skills and shooting touch.

So, what might some of those other things be? Well, suppose that instead of measuring your IQ, I gave you a totally different kind of test.

Write down as many different uses that you can think of for the following objects:

1. a brick
2. a blanket

This is an example of what's called a "divergence test" (as opposed to a test like the Raven's, which asks you to sort through a list of possibilities and *converge* on the right answer). It requires you to use your imagination and take your mind in as many different directions as possible. With a divergence test, obviously there isn't a single right answer. What the test giver is looking for are the number and the uniqueness of your responses. And what the test is measuring isn't analytical intelligence but something profoundly different— something much closer to creativity. Divergence tests are every bit as challenging as convergence tests, and if you don't believe that, I encourage you to pause and try the brick-and-blanket test right now.

Here, for example, are answers to the "uses of objects" test collected by Liam Hudson from a student named Poole at a top British high school:

(Brick). To use in smash-and-grab raids. To help hold a house together. To use in a game of Russian roulette if you want to keep fit at the same time (bricks at ten paces, turn and throw—no evasive action allowed). To hold the eiderdown on a bed tie a brick at each corner. As a breaker of empty Coca-Cola bottles.

(Blanket). To use on a bed. As a cover for illicit sex in the woods. As a tent. To make smoke signals with. As a sail for a boat, cart or sled. As a substitute for a towel. As a target for shooting practice for short-sighted people. As a thing to catch people jumping out of burning skyscrapers.

It's not hard to read Poole's answers and get some sense of how his mind works. He's funny. He's a little subversive and libidinous. He has the flair for the dramatic. His mind leaps from violent imagery to sex to people jumping out of burning skyscrapers to very practical issues, such as how to get a duvet to stay on a bed. He gives us the impression that if we gave him another ten minutes, he'd come up with another twenty uses.[*]

Now, for the sake of comparison, consider the answers of another student from Hudson's sample. His name is Florence. Hudson tells us that Florence is a prodigy, with one of the highest IQs in his school.

(Brick). Building things, throwing.

(Blanket). Keeping warm, smothering fire, tying to trees and sleeping in (as a hammock), improvised stretcher.

Where is Florence's imagination? He identified the most common and most functional uses for bricks and blankets and simply stopped. Florence's IQ is higher than Poole's. But that means little, since both students are above the threshold. What is more interesting is that Poole's mind can leap from violent imagery to sex to people jumping out of buildings without missing a beat, and Florence's mind can't. Now which of these two students do you think is better suited to do the kind of brilliant, imaginative work that wins Nobel Prizes? That's the second reason Nobel Prize winners come from Holy Cross as well as Harvard, because Harvard isn't selecting its students on the basis of how well they do on the "uses of a brick" test—and maybe "uses of a brick" is a better predictor of Nobel Prize ability. It's also the second reason Michigan Law School couldn't find a difference between its affirmative action graduates and the rest of its alumni. Being a successful lawyer is about a lot more than IQ. It involves having the kind of fertile mind that Poole had. And just because Michigan's minority students have lower scores on convergence tests doesn't mean they don't have that other critical trait in abundance.

5.

This was Terman's error. He fell in love with the fact that his Termites were at the absolute pinnacle of the intellectual scale—at the ninety-ninth percentile of the ninety-ninth percentile—without realizing how little that seemingly extraordinary fact meant.

By the time the Termites reached adulthood, Terman's error was plain to see. Some of his child geniuses had grown up to publish books and scholarly articles and thrive in business. Several ran for public office, and there were two superior court justices, one municipal court judge, two members of the California state legislature, and one prominent state official. But few of his geniuses were nationally known figures. They tended to earn good incomes—but not *that* good. The majority had careers that could only be considered ordinary, and a surprising number ended up with careers that even Terman considered failures. Nor were there any Nobel Prize winners in his exhaustively selected group of geniuses. His fieldworkers actually tested two elementary students who went on to be Nobel laureates—William Shockley and Luis Alvarez—and rejected them both. Their IQs weren't high enough.

In a devastating critique, the sociologist Pitirim Sorokin once showed that if Terman had simply put together a randomly selected group of children from the same kinds of family backgrounds as the Termites—and dispensed with IQs altogether—he would have ended up with a group doing almost as many impressive things as his painstakingly selected group of geniuses. "By no stretch of the imagination or of standards of genius," Sorokin concluded, "is the 'gifted group' as a whole 'gifted.'" By the time Terman came out with his fourth volume of *Genetic Studies of Genius*, the word "genius" had all but vanished. "We have seen," Terman concluded, with more than a touch of disappointment, "that intellect and achievement are far from perfectly correlated."

What I told you at the beginning of this chapter about the extraordinary intelligence of Chris Langan, in other words, is of little use if we want to understand his chances of being a success in the world. Yes, he is a man with a one-in-a-million mind and the ability to get through *Principia Mathematica* at sixteen. And yes, his sentences come marching out one after another, polished and crisp like soldiers on a parade ground. But so what? If we want to understand the likelihood of his becoming a true outlier, we have to know a lot more about him than that.

CHAPTER FOUR

The Trouble with Geniuses, Part 2

"AFTER PROTRACTED NEGOTIATIONS. IT WAS AGREED THAT ROBERT WOULD BE

1.

Chris Langan's mother was from San Francisco and was estranged from her family. She had four sons, each with a different father. Chris was the eldest. His father disappeared before Chris was born; he was said to have died in Mexico. His mother's second husband was murdered. Her third committed suicide. Her fourth was a failed journalist named Jack Langan.

"To this day I haven't met anybody who was as poor when they were kids as our family was," Chris Langan says. "We didn't have a pair of matched socks. Our shoes had holes in them. Our pants had holes in them. We only had one set of clothes. I remember my brothers and I going into the bathroom and using the bathtub to wash our only set of clothes and we were bare-assed naked when we were doing that because we didn't have anything to wear."

Jack Langan would go on drinking sprees and disappear. He would lock the kitchen cabinets so the boys couldn't get to the food. He used a bullwhip to keep the boys in line. He would get jobs and then lose them, moving the family on to the next town. One summer the family lived on an Indian reservation in a teepee, subsisting on government-surplus peanut butter and cornmeal. For a time, they lived in Virginia City, Nevada. "There was only one law officer in town, and when the Hell's Angels came to town, he would crouch down in the back of his office," Mark Langan remembers. "There was a bar there, I'll always remember. It was called the Bucket of Blood Saloon."

When the boys were in grade school, the family moved to Bozeman, Montana. One of Chris's brothers spent time in a foster home. Another was sent to reform school.

"I don't think the school ever understood just how gifted Christopher was," his brother Jeff says. "He sure as hell didn't play it up. This was Bozeman. It wasn't like it is today. It was a small hick town when we were growing up. We weren't treated well there. They'd just decided that my family was a bunch of deadbeats." To stick up for himself and his brothers, Chris started to lift weights.

One day, when Chris was fourteen, Jack Langan got rough with the boys, as he sometimes did, and Chris knocked him out cold. Jack left, never to return. Upon graduation from high school, Chris was offered two full scholarships, one to Reed College in Oregon and the other to the University of Chicago. He chose Reed.

"It was a huge mistake," Chris recalls. "I had a real case of culture shock. I was a crew-cut kid who had been working as a ranch hand in the summers in Montana, and there I was, with a whole bunch of long-haired city kids, most of them from New York. And these kids had a whole different style than I was used to. I couldn't get a word in edgewise at class. They were very inquisitive. Asking questions all the time. I was crammed into a dorm room. There were four of us, and the other three guys had a whole different other lifestyle. They were smoking pot. They would bring their girlfriends into the room. I had never smoked pot before. So basically I took to hiding in the library."

He continued: "Then I lost that scholarship…. My mother was supposed to fill out a parents' financial statement for the renewal of that scholarship. She neglected to do so. She was confused by the requirements or whatever. At some point, it came to my attention that my scholarship had not been renewed. So I went to the office to ask why, and they told me, Well, no one sent us the financial statement, and we allocated all the scholarship money and it's all gone, so I'm afraid that you don't have a scholarship here anymore. That was the style of the place. They simply didn't care. They didn't give a shit about their students. There was no counseling, no mentoring, nothing."

Chris left Reed before the final set of exams, leaving him with a row of Fs on his transcript. In the first semester, he had earned As. He went back to Bozeman and worked in construction and as a forest services firefighter for a year and a half. Then he enrolled at Montana State University.

"I was taking math and philosophy classes," he recalled. "And then in the winter quarter, I was living thirteen miles out of town, out on Beach Hill Road, and the transmission fell out of my car. My brothers had used it when I was gone that summer. They were working for the railroad and had driven it on the railroad tracks. I didn't have the money to repair it. So I went to my adviser and the dean in sequence and said, I have a problem. The transmission fell out of my car, and you have me in a seven-thirty a.m. and eight-thirty a.m. class. If you could please just transfer me to the afternoon sections of these classes, I would appreciate it because of this car problem. There was a neighbor who was a rancher who was going to take me in at eleven o'clock. My adviser was this cowboy-looking guy with a handlebar mustache, dressed in a tweed jacket. He said, 'Well, son, after looking at your transcript at Reed College, I see that you have yet to learn that everyone has to make sacrifices to get an education. Request denied.' So then I went to the dean. Same treatment."

His voice grew tight. He was describing things that had happened more than thirty years ago, but the memory still made him angry. "At that point I realized, here I was, knocking myself out to make the money to make my way back to school, and it's the middle of the Montana winter. I am willing to hitchhike into town every day, do whatever I had to do, just to get into school and back, and they are unwilling to do anything for me. So bananas. And that was the point I decided I could do without the higher-education system. Even if I couldn't do without it, it was sufficiently repugnant to me that I wouldn't do it anymore. So I dropped out of college, simple as that."

Chris Langan's experiences at Reed and Montana State represented a turning point in his life. As a child, he had dreamt of becoming an academic. He *should* have gotten a PhD; universities are institutions structured, in large part, for people with his kind of deep intellectual interests and curiosity. "Once he got into the university environment, I thought he would prosper, I really did," his brother Mark says. "I thought he would somehow find a niche. It made absolutely no sense to me when he left that."

Without a degree, Langan floundered. He worked in construction. One frigid winter he worked on a clam boat on Long Island. He took factory jobs and minor civil service positions and eventually became a bouncer in a bar on Long Island, which was his principal occupation for much of his adult years. Through it all, he continued to read deeply in philosophy, mathematics, and physics as he worked on a sprawling treatise he calls the "CTMU"—the "Cognitive Theoretic Model of the Universe." But without academic credentials, he despairs of ever getting published in a scholarly journal.

"I am a guy who has a year and a half of college," he says, with a shrug. "And at some point this will come to the attention of the editor, as he is going to take the paper and send it off to the referees, and these referees are going to try and look me up, and they are not going to find me. And they are going to say, This guy has a year and a half of college. How can he know what he's talking about?"

It is a heartbreaking story. At one point I asked Langan—hypothetically—whether he would take a job at Harvard University were it offered to him. "Well, that's a difficult question," he replied. "Obviously, as a full professor at Harvard

I would count. My ideas would have weight and I could use my position, my affiliation at Harvard, to promote my ideas. An institution like that is a great source of intellectual energy, and if I were at a place like that, I could absorb the vibration in the air." It was suddenly clear how lonely his life has been. Here he was, a man with an insatiable appetite for learning, forced for most of his adult life to live in intellectual isolation. "I even noticed that kind of intellectual energy in the year and a half I was in college," he said, almost wistfully. "Ideas are in the air constantly. It's such a stimulating place to be.

"On the other hand," he went on, "Harvard is basically a glorified corporation, operating with a profit incentive. That's what makes it tick. It has an endowment in the billions of dollars. The people running it are not necessarily searching for truth and knowledge. They want to be big shots, and when you accept a paycheck from these people, it is going to come down to what you want to do and what you feel is right versus what the man says you can do to receive another paycheck. When you're there, they got a thumb right on you. They are out to make sure you don't step out of line."

2.

What does the story of Chris Langan tell us? His explanations, as heartbreaking as they are, are also a little strange. His mother forgets to sign his financial aid form and—just like that—no scholarship. He tries to move from a morning to an afternoon class, something students do every day, and gets stopped cold. And why were Langan's teachers at Reed and Montana State so indifferent to his plight? Teachers typically delight in minds as brilliant as his. Langan talks about dealing with Reed and Montana State as if they were some kind of vast and unyielding government bureaucracy. But colleges, particularly small liberal arts colleges like Reed, tend not to be rigid bureaucracies. Making allowances in the name of helping someone stay in school is what professors do all the time.

Even in his discussion of Harvard, it's as if Langan has no conception of the culture and particulars of the institution he's talking about. *When you accept a paycheck from these people, it is going to come down to what you want to do and what you feel is right versus what the man says you can do to receive another paycheck.* What? One of the main reasons college professors accept a lower paycheck than they could get in private industry is that university life gives them the freedom to do what they want to do and what they feel is right. Langan has

Harvard backwards.

When Langan told me his life story, I couldn't help thinking of the life of Robert Oppenheimer, the physicist who famously headed the American effort to develop the nuclear bomb during World War II. Oppenheimer, by all accounts, was a child with a mind very much like Chris Langan's. His parents considered him a genius. One of his teachers recalled that "he received every new idea as perfectly beautiful." He was doing lab experiments by the third grade and studying physics and chemistry by the fifth grade. When he was nine, he once told one of his cousins, "Ask me a question in Latin and I will answer you in Greek."

Oppenheimer went to Harvard and then on to Cambridge University to pursue a doctorate in physics. There, Oppenheimer, who struggled with depression his entire life, grew despondent. His gift was for theoretical physics, and his tutor, a man named Patrick Blackett (who would win a Nobel Prize in 1948), was forcing him to attend to the minutiae of experimental physics, which he hated. He grew more and more emotionally unstable, and then, in an act so strange that to this day no one has properly made sense of it, Oppenheimer took some chemicals from the laboratory and tried to poison his tutor.

Blackett, luckily, found out that something was amiss. The university was informed. Oppenheimer was called on the carpet. And what happened next is every bit as unbelievable as the crime itself. Here is how the incident is described in *American Prometheus*, Kai Bird and Martin Sherwin's biography of Oppenheimer: "After protracted negotiations, it was agreed that Robert would be put on probation and have regular sessions with a prominent Harley Street psychiatrist in London."

On probation?

Here we have two very brilliant young students, each of whom runs into a problem that imperils his college career. Langan's mother has missed a deadline for his financial aid. Oppenheimer has tried to poison his tutor. To continue on, they are required to plead their cases to authority. And what happens? Langan gets his scholarship taken away, and Oppenheimer gets sent to a psychiatrist. Oppenheimer and Langan might both be geniuses, but in other ways, they could not be more different.

The story of Oppenheimer's appointment to be scientific director of the Manhattan Project twenty years later is perhaps an even better example of this difference. The general in charge of the Manhattan Project was Leslie Groves, and he scoured the country, trying to find the right person to lead the atomic-bomb effort. Oppenheimer, by rights, was a long shot. He was just thirty-eight, and junior to many of the people whom he would have to manage. He was a theorist, and this was a job that called for experimenters and engineers. His political affiliations were dodgy: he had all kinds of friends who were Communists. Perhaps more striking, he had never had any administrative experience. "He was a very impractical fellow," one of Oppenheimer's friends later said. "He walked about with scuffed shoes and a funny hat, and, more important, he didn't know anything about equipment." As one Berkeley scientist put it, more succinctly: "He couldn't run a hamburger stand."

Oh, and by the way, in graduate school *he tried to kill his tutor*. This was the résumé of the man who was trying out for what might be said to be—without exaggeration—one of the most important jobs of the twentieth century. And what happened? The same thing that happened twenty years earlier at Cambridge: he got the rest of the world to see things his way.

Here are Bird and Sherwin again: "Oppenheimer understood that Groves guarded the entrance to the Manhattan Project, and he therefore turned on all his charm and brilliance. It was an irresistible performance." Groves was smitten. " 'He's a genius,' Groves later told a reporter. 'A real genius.' " Groves was an engineer by training with a graduate degree from MIT, and Oppenheimer's great insight was to appeal to that side of Groves. Bird and Sherwin go on: "Oppenheimer was the first scientist Groves had met on his tour [of potential candidates] who grasped that building an atomic bomb required finding practical solutions to a variety of cross-disciplinary problems.... [Groves] found himself nodding in agreement when Oppenheimer pitched the notion of a central laboratory devoted to this purpose, where, as he later testified, 'we could begin to come to grips with chemical, metallurgical, engineering and ordnance problems that had so far received no consideration.' "

Would Oppenheimer have lost his scholarship at Reed? Would he have been unable to convince his professors to move his classes to the afternoon? Of course not. And that's not because he was smarter than Chris Langan. It's because he possessed the kind of savvy that allowed him to get what he wanted from the world.

"They required that everyone take introductory calculus," Langan said of his brief stay at Montana State. "And I happened to get a guy who taught it in a very dry, very trivial way. I didn't understand why he was teaching it this way. So I asked him questions. I actually had to chase him down to his office. I asked him, 'Why are you teaching this way? Why do you consider this practice to be relevant to calculus?' And this guy, this tall, lanky guy, always had sweat stains under his arms, he turned and looked at me and said, 'You know, there is something you should probably get straight. Some people just don't have the intellectual firepower to be mathematicians.' ''

There they are, the professor and the prodigy, and what the prodigy clearly wants is to be engaged, at long last, with a mind that loves mathematics as much as he does. But he fails. In fact—and this is the most heartbreaking part of all—he manages to have an entire conversation with his calculus professor without ever communicating the one fact most likely to appeal to a calculus professor. The professor never realizes that Chris Langan is good at calculus.

3.

The particular skill that allows you to talk your way out of a murder rap, or convince your professor to move you from the morning to the afternoon section, is what the psychologist Robert Sternberg calls "practical intelligence." To Sternberg, practical intelligence includes things like "knowing what to say to whom, knowing when to say it, and knowing how to say it for maximum effect." It is procedural: it is about knowing *how* to do something without necessarily knowing why you know it or being able to explain it. It's practical in nature: that is, it's not knowledge for its own sake. It's knowledge that helps you read situations correctly and get what you want. And, critically, it is a kind of intelligence separate from the sort of analytical ability measured by IQ. To use the technical term, general intelligence and practical intelligence are "orthogonal": the presence of one doesn't imply the presence of the other. You can have lots of analytical intelligence and very little practical intelligence, or lots of practical intelligence and not much analytical intelligence, or—as in the lucky case of someone like Robert Oppenheimer—you can have lots of both.

So where does something like practical intelligence come from? We know where analytical intelligence comes from. It's something, at least in part, that's in your genes. Chris Langan started talking at six months. He taught himself to read at three years of age. He was *born* smart. IQ is a measure, to some degree, of innate ability.* But social savvy is *knowledge.* It's a set of skills that have to be learned. It has to come from somewhere, and the place where we seem to get these kinds of attitudes and skills is from our families.

Perhaps the best explanation we have of this process comes from the sociologist Annette Lareau, who a few years ago conducted a fascinating study of a group of third graders. She picked both blacks and whites and children from both wealthy homes and poor homes, zeroing in, ultimately, on twelve families. Lareau and her team visited each family at least twenty times, for hours at a stretch. She and her assistants told their subjects to treat them like "the family dog," and they followed them to church and to soccer games and to doctor's appointments, with a tape recorder in one hand and a notebook in the other.

You might expect that if you spent such an extended period in twelve different households, what you would gather is twelve different ideas about how to raise children: there would be the strict parents and the lax parents and the hyperinvolved parents and the mellow parents and on and on. What Lareau found, however, is something much different. There were only two parenting "philosophies," and they divided almost perfectly along class lines. The wealthier parents raised their kids one way, and the poorer parents raised their kids another way.

The wealthier parents were heavily involved in their children's free time, shuttling them from one activity to the next, quizzing them about their teachers and coaches and teammates. One of the well-off children Lareau followed played on a baseball team, two soccer teams, a swim team, and a basketball team in the summer, as well as playing in an orchestra and taking piano lessons.

That kind of intensive scheduling was almost entirely absent from the lives of the poor children. Play for them wasn't soccer practice twice a week. It was making up games outside with their siblings and other kids in the neighborhood. What a child did was considered by his or her parents as something separate from the adult world and not particularly consequential. One girl from a working-class family—Katie Brindle—sang in a choir after school. But she signed up for it herself and walked to choir practice on her own. Lareau writes:

> What Mrs. Brindle doesn't do that is routine for middle-class mothers is view her daughter's interest in singing as a signal to look for other ways to help her develop that interest into a formal talent. Similarly Mrs. Brindle does not discuss Katie's interest in drama or express regret that she cannot afford to cultivate her daughter's talent. Instead she frames Katie's skills and interests as character traits—singing and acting are part of what makes Katie "Katie." She sees the shows her daughter puts on as "cute" and as a way for Katie to "get attention."

The middle-class parents talked things through with their children, reasoning with them. They didn't just issue commands. They expected their children to talk back to them, to negotiate, to question adults in positions of authority. If their children were doing poorly at school, the wealthier parents challenged their teachers. They intervened on behalf of their kids. One child Lareau follows just misses qualifying for a gifted program. Her mother arranges for her to be retested privately, petitions the school, and gets her daughter admitted. The poor parents, by contrast, are intimidated by authority. They react passively and stay in the background. Lareau writes of one low-income parent:

> At a parent-teacher conference, for example, Ms. McAllister (who is a high school graduate) seems subdued. The gregarious and outgoing nature she displays at home is hidden in this setting. She sits hunched over in the chair and she keeps her jacket zipped up. She is very quiet. When the teacher reports that Harold has not been turning in his homework, Ms. McAllister clearly is flabbergasted, but all she says is, "He did it at home." She does not follow up with the teacher or attempt to intervene on Harold's behalf. In her view, it is up to the teachers to manage her son's education. That is their job, not hers.

Lareau calls the middle-class parenting style "concerted cultivation." It's an attempt to actively "foster and assess a child's talents, opinions and skills." Poor parents tend to follow, by contrast, a strategy of "accomplishment of natural growth." They see as their responsibility to care for their children but to let them grow and develop on their own.

Lareau stresses that one style isn't morally better than the other. The poorer children were, to her mind, often better behaved, less whiny, more creative in making use of their own time, and had a well-developed sense of independence. But in practical terms, concerted cultivation has enormous advantages. The heavily scheduled middle-class child is exposed to a constantly shifting set of experiences. She learns teamwork and how to cope in highly structured settings. She is taught how to interact comfortably with adults, and to speak up when she needs to. In Lareau's words, the middle-class children learn a sense of "entitlement."

That word, of course, has negative connotations these days. But Lareau means it in the best sense of the term: "They acted as though they had a right to pursue their own individual preferences and to actively manage interactions in institutional settings. They appeared comfortable in those settings; they were open to sharing information and asking for attention…. It was common practice among middle-class children to shift interactions to suit their preferences." They knew the rules. "Even in fourth grade, middle-class children appeared to be acting on their own behalf to gain advantages. They made special requests of teachers and doctors to adjust procedures to accommodate their desires."

By contrast, the working-class and poor children were characterized by "an emerging sense of distance, distrust, and constraint." They didn't know how to get their way, or how to "customize"—using Lareau's wonderful term—whatever environment they were in, for their best purposes.

In one telling scene, Lareau describes a visit to the doctor by Alex Williams, a nine-year-old boy, and his mother, Christina. The Williamses are wealthy professionals.

"Alex, you should be thinking of questions you might want to ask the doctor," Christina says in the car on the way to the doctor's office. "You can ask him anything you want. Don't be shy. You can ask anything."

Alex thinks for a minute, then says, "I have some bumps under my arms from my deodorant." Christina: "Really? You mean from your new deodorant?" Alex: "Yes." Christina: "Well, you should ask the doctor."

Alex's mother, Lareau writes, "is teaching that he has the right to speak up"—that even though he's going to be in a room with an older person and authority figure, it's perfectly all right for him to assert himself. They meet the doctor, a genial man in his early forties. He tells Alex that he is in the ninety-fifth percentile in height. Alex then interrupts:

ALEX: I'm in the what?
DOCTOR: It means that you're taller than more than ninety-five out of a
    hundred young men when they're, uh, ten years old.
ALEX: I'm not ten.
DOCTOR: Well, they graphed you at ten. You're—nine years and ten months.
    They—they usually take the closest year to that graph.

Look at how easily Alex interrupts the doctor—"I'm not ten." That's entitlement: his mother permits that casual incivility because she wants him to learn to assert himself with people in positions of authority.

THE DOCTOR TURNS TO ALEX: Well, now the most important question. Do you
    have any questions you want to ask me before I do your physical?
ALEX: Um… only one. I've been getting some bumps on my arms, right
    around here (indicates underarm).
DOCTOR: Underneath?
ALEX: Yeah.
DOCTOR: Okay. I'll have to take a look at those when I come in closer to do
    the checkup. And I'll see what they are and what I can do. Do they hurt or
    itch?
ALEX: No, they're just there.
DOCTOR: Okay, I'll take a look at those bumps for you.

This kind of interaction simply doesn't happen with lower-class children,
Lareau says. They would be quiet and submissive, with eyes turned away. Alex
takes charge of the moment. "In remembering to raise the question he prepared
in advance, he gains the doctor's full attention and focuses it on an issue of his
choosing," Lareau writes.

In so doing, he successfully shifts the balance of power away from the
adults and toward himself. The transition goes smoothly. Alex is used to
being treated with respect. He is seen as special and as a person worthy of
adult attention and interest. These are key characteristics of the strategy of
concerted cultivation. Alex is not showing off during his checkup. He is
behaving much as he does with his parents—he reasons, negotiates, and
jokes with equal ease.

It is important to understand where the particular mastery of that moment
comes from. It's not genetic. Alex Williams didn't inherit the skills to interact
with authority figures from his parents and grandparents the way he inherited the
color of his eyes. Nor is it racial: it's not a practice specific to either black or
white people. As it turns out, Alex Williams is black and Katie Brindle is white.
It's a *cultural* advantage. Alex has those skills because over the course of his
young life, his mother and father—in the manner of educated families—have
painstakingly taught them to him, nudging and prodding and encouraging and
showing him the rules of the game, right down to that little rehearsal in the car

on the way to the doctor's office.

When we talk about the advantages of class, Lareau argues, this is in large part what we mean. Alex Williams is better off than Katie Brindle because he's wealthier and because he goes to a better school, but also because—and perhaps this is even more critical—the sense of entitlement that he has been taught is an attitude perfectly suited to succeeding in the modern world.

4.

This is the advantage that Oppenheimer had and that Chris Langan lacked. Oppenheimer was raised in one of the wealthiest neighborhoods in Manhattan, the son of an artist and a successful garment manufacturer. His childhood was the embodiment of concerted cultivation. On weekends, the Oppenheimers would go driving in the countryside in a chauffeur-driven Packard. Summers he would be taken to Europe to see his grandfather. He attended the Ethical Culture School on Central Park West, perhaps the most progressive school in the nation, where, his biographers write, students were "infused with the notion that they were being groomed to reform the world." When his math teacher realized he was bored, she sent him off to do independent work.

As a child, Oppenheimer was passionate about rock collecting. At the age of twelve, he began corresponding with local geologists about rock formations he had seen in Central Park, and he so impressed them that they invited him to give a lecture before the New York Mineralogical Club. As Sherwin and Bird write, Oppenheimer's parents responded to their son's hobby in an almost textbook example of concerted cultivation:

> Dreading the thought of having to talk to an audience of adults, Robert begged his father to explain that they had invited a twelve-year-old. Greatly amused, Julius encouraged his son to accept this honor. On the designated evening, Robert showed up at the club with his parents, who proudly introduced their son as J. Robert Oppenheimer. The startled audience of geologists and amateur rock collectors burst out laughing when he stepped up to the podium: a wooden box had to be found for him to stand on so that the audience could see more than the shock of his wiry black hair sticking up above the lectern. Shy and awkward, Robert

nevertheless read his prepared remarks and was given a hearty round of applause.

Is it any wonder Oppenheimer handled the challenges of his life so brilliantly? If you are someone whose father has made his way up in the business world, then you've seen, firsthand, what it means to negotiate your way out of a tight spot. If you're someone who was sent to the Ethical Culture School, then you aren't going to be intimidated by a row of Cambridge dons arrayed in judgment against you. If you studied physics at Harvard, then you know how to talk to an army general who did engineering just down the road at MIT.

Chris Langan, by contrast, had only the bleakness of Bozeman, and a home dominated by an angry, drunken stepfather. "[Jack] Langan did this to all of us," said Mark. "We all have a true resentment of authority." That was the lesson Langan learned from his childhood: distrust authority and be independent. He never had a parent teach him on the way to the doctor how to speak up for himself, or how to reason and negotiate with those in positions of authority. He didn't learn entitlement. He learned constraint. It may seem like a small thing, but it was a crippling handicap in navigating the world beyond Bozeman.

"I couldn't get any financial aid either," Mark went on. "We just had zero knowledge, less than zero knowledge, of the process. How to apply. The forms. Checkbooks. It was not our environment."

"If Christopher had been born into a wealthy family, if he was the son of a doctor who was well connected in some major market, I guarantee you he would have been one of those guys you read about, knocking back PhDs at seventeen," his brother Jeff says. "It's the culture you find yourself in that determines that. The issue with Chris is that he was always too bored to actually sit there and listen to his teachers. If someone had recognized his intelligence and if he was from a family where there was some kind of value on education, they would have made sure he wasn't bored."

5.

When the Termites were into their adulthood, Terman looked at the records of 730 of the men and divided them into three groups. One hundred and fifty—the top 20 percent—fell into what Terman called the A group. They were the true success stories, the stars—the lawyers and physicians and engineers and academics. Ninety percent of the As graduated from college and among them had earned 98 graduate degrees. The middle 60 percent were the B group, those who were doing "satisfactorily." The bottom 150 were the Cs, the ones who Terman judged to have done the least with their superior mental ability. They were the postal workers and the struggling bookkeepers and the men lying on their couches at home without any job at all.

One third of the Cs were college dropouts. A quarter only had a high school diploma, and all 150 of the Cs—each one of whom, at one point in his life, had been dubbed a genius—had together earned a grand total of eight graduate degrees.

What was the difference between the As and the Cs? Terman ran through every conceivable explanation. He looked at their physical and mental health, their "masculinity-femininity scores," and their hobbies and vocational interests. He compared the ages when they started walking and talking and what their precise IQ scores were in elementary and high school. In the end, only one thing mattered: family background.

The As overwhelmingly came from the middle and the upper class. Their homes were filled with books. Half the fathers of the A group had a college degree or beyond, and this at a time when a university education was a rarity. The Cs, on the other hand, were from the other side of the tracks. Almost a third of them had a parent who had dropped out of school before the eighth grade.

At one point, Terman had his fieldworkers go and visit everyone from the A and C groups and rate their personalities and manner. What they found is everything you would expect to find if you were comparing children raised in an atmosphere of concerted cultivation with children raised in an atmosphere of natural growth. The As were judged to be much more alert, poised, attractive, and well dressed. In fact, the scores on those four dimensions are so different as to make you think you are looking at two different species of humans. You aren't, of course. You're simply seeing the difference between those schooled by their families to present their best face to the world, and those denied that experience.

The Terman results are deeply distressing. Let's not forget how highly gifted the C group was. If you had met them at five or six years of age, you would have been overwhelmed by their curiosity and mental agility and sparkle. They were true outliers. The plain truth of the Terman study, however, is that in the end almost *none* of the genius children from the lowest social and economic class ended up making a name for themselves.

What did the Cs lack, though? Not something expensive or impossible to find; not something encoded in DNA or hardwired into the circuits of their brains. They lacked something that could have been given to them if we'd only known they needed it: a community around them that prepared them properly for the world. The Cs were squandered talent. But they didn't need to be.

6.

Today, Chris Langan lives in rural Missouri on a horse farm. He moved there a few years ago, after he got married. He is in his fifties but looks many years younger. He has the build of a linebacker, thick through the chest, with enormous biceps. His hair is combed straight back from his forehead. He has a neat, graying moustache and aviator-style glasses. If you look into his eyes, you can see the intelligence burning behind them.

"A typical day is, I get up and make coffee. I go in and sit in front of the computer and begin working on whatever I was working on the night before," he told me not long ago. "I found if I go to bed with a question on my mind, all I have to do is concentrate on the question before I go to sleep and I virtually always have the answer in the morning. Sometimes I realize what the answer is because I dreamt the answer and I can remember it. Other times I just feel the answer, and I start typing and the answer emerges onto the page."

He had just been reading the work of the linguist Noam Chomsky. There were piles of books in his study. He ordered books from the library all the time. "I always feel that the closer you get to the original sources, the better off you are," he said.

Langan seemed content. He had farm animals to take care of, and books to read, and a wife he loved. It was a much better life than being a bouncer.

"I don't think there is anyone smarter than me out there," he went on. "I have never met anybody like me or never seen even an indication that there is somebody who actually has better powers of comprehension. Never seen it and I don't think I am going to. I could—my mind is open to the possibility. If anyone should challenge me—'Oh, I think that I am smarter than you are'—I think I could have them."

What he said sounded boastful, but it wasn't really. It was the opposite—a touch defensive. He'd been working for decades now on a project of enormous sophistication—but almost none of what he had done had ever been published much less read by the physicists and philosophers and mathematicians who might be able to judge its value. Here he was, a man with a one-in-a-million mind, and he had yet to have any impact on the world. He wasn't holding forth at academic conferences. He wasn't leading a graduate seminar at some prestigious university. He was living on a slightly tumbledown horse farm in northern Missouri, sitting on the back porch in jeans and a cutoff T-shirt. He knew how it looked: it was the great paradox of Chris Langan's genius.

"I have not pursued mainstream publishers as hard as I should have," he conceded. "Going around, querying publishers, trying to find an agent. I haven't done it, and I am not interested in doing it."

It was an admission of defeat. Every experience he had had outside of his own mind had ended in frustration. He knew he needed to do a better job of navigating the world, but he didn't know how. He couldn't even talk to his calculus teacher, for goodness' sake. These were things that others, with lesser minds, could master easily. But that's because those others had had help along the way, and Chris Langan never had. It wasn't an excuse. It was a fact. He'd had to make his way alone, and no one—not rock stars, not professional athletes, not software billionaires, and not even geniuses—ever makes it alone.

CHAPTER FIVE

The Three Lessons of Joe Flom

"MARY GOT A QUARTER."

1.

Joe Flom is the last living "named" partner of the law firm Skadden, Arps, Slate, Meagher and Flom. He has a corner office high atop the Condé Nast tower in Manhattan. He is short and slightly hunched. His head is large, framed by long prominent ears, and his narrow blue eyes are hidden by oversize aviator-style glasses. He is slender now, but during his heyday, Flom was extremely overweight. He waddles when he walks. He doodles when he thinks. He mumbles when he talks, and when he makes his way down the halls of Skadden, Arps, conversations drop to a hush.

Flom grew up in the Depression in Brooklyn's Borough Park neighborhood. His parents were Jewish immigrants from Eastern Europe. His father, Isadore, was a union organizer in the garment industry who later went to work sewing shoulder pads for ladies' dresses. His mother worked at what was called piecework—doing appliqué at home. They were desperately poor. His family moved nearly every year when he was growing up because the custom in those days was for landlords to give new tenants a month's free rent, and without that, his family could not get by.

In junior high school, Flom took the entrance exam for the elite Townsend Harris public high school on Lexington Avenue in Manhattan, a school that in just forty years of existence produced three Nobel Prize winners, six Pulitzer Prize winners, and one Supreme Court Justice, not to mention George Gershwin and Jonas Salk, the inventor of the polio vaccine. He got in. His mother would give him a dime in the morning for breakfast—three donuts, orange juice, and coffee at Nedick's. After school, he pushed a hand truck in the garment district.

He did two years of night school at City College in upper Manhattan—working during the days to make ends meet—signed up for the army, served his time, and applied to Harvard Law School.

"I wanted to get into the law since I was six years old," Flom says. He didn't have a degree from college. Harvard took him anyway. "Why? I wrote them a letter on why I was the answer to sliced bread," is how Flom explains it, with characteristic brevity. At Harvard, in the late 1940s, he never took notes. "All of us were going through this first year idiocy of writing notes carefully in the classroom and doing an outline of that, then a condensation of that, and then doing it again on onionskin paper, on top of other paper," remembers Charles Haar, who was a classmate of Flom's. "It was a routinized way of trying to learn the cases. Not Joe. He wouldn't have any of that. But he had that quality which we always vaguely subsumed under 'thinking like a lawyer.' He had the great capacity for judgment."

Flom was named to the *Law Review*—an honor reserved for the very top students in the class. During "hiring season," the Christmas break of his second year, he went down to New York to interview with the big corporate law firms of the day. "I was ungainly, awkward, a fat kid. I didn't feel comfortable," Flom remembers. "I was one of two kids in my class at the end of hiring season who didn't have a job. Then one day, one of my professors said that there are these guys starting a firm. I had a visit with them, and the entire time I met with them, they were telling me what the risks were of going with a firm that didn't have a client. The more they talked, the more I liked them. So I said, What the hell, I'll take a chance. They had to scrape together the thirty-six hundred a year, which was the starting salary." In the beginning, it was just Marshall Skadden, Leslie Arps—both of whom had just been turned down for partner at a major Wall Street law firm—and John Slate, who had worked for Pan Am airlines. Flom was their associate. They had a tiny suite of offices on the top floor of the Lehman Brothers Building on Wall Street. "What kind of law did we do?" Flom says, laughing. "Whatever came in the door!"

In 1954, Flom took over as Skadden's managing partner, and the firm began to grow by leaps and bounds. Soon it had one hundred lawyers. Then two hundred. When it hit three hundred, one of Flom's partners—Morris Kramer—came to him and said that he felt guilty about bringing in young law school graduates. Skadden was so big, Kramer said, that it was hard to imagine the firm growing beyond that and being able to promote any of those hires. Flom told him, "Ahhh, we'll go to one thousand." Flom never lacked for ambition.

Today Skadden, Arps has nearly two thousand attorneys in twenty-three offices around the world and earns well over $1 billion a year, making it one of the largest and most powerful law firms in the world. In his office, Flom has pictures of himself with George Bush Sr. and Bill Clinton. He lives in a sprawling apartment in a luxurious building on Manhattan's Upper East Side. For a period of almost thirty years, if you were a Fortune 500 company about to be taken over or trying to take over someone else, or merely a big shot in some kind of fix, Joseph Flom has been your attorney and Skadden, Arps has been your law firm—and if they weren't, you probably wished they were.

2.

I hope by now that you are skeptical of this kind of story. Brilliant immigrant kid overcomes poverty and the Depression, can't get a job at the stuffy downtown law firms, makes it on his own through sheer hustle and ability. It's a rags-to-riches story, and everything we've learned so far from hockey players and software billionaires and the Termites suggests that success doesn't happen that way. Successful people don't do it alone. Where they come from matters. They're products of particular places and environments.

Just as we did, then, with Bill Joy and Chris Langan, let's start over with Joseph Flom, this time putting to use everything we've learned from the first four chapters of this book. No more talk of Joe Flom's intelligence, or personality, or ambition, though he obviously has these three things in abundance. No glowing quotations from his clients, testifying to his genius. No more colorful tales from the meteoric rise of Skadden, Arps, Slate, Meagher and Flom.

Instead, I'm going to tell a series of stories from the New York immigrant world that Joe Flom grew up in—of a fellow law student, a father and son named Maurice and Mort Janklow, and an extraordinary couple by the name of Louis and Regina Borgenicht—in the hopes of answering a critical question. What were Joe Flom's opportunities? Since we know that outliers always have help along the way, can we sort through the ecology of Joe Flom and identify the conditions that helped create him?

We tell rags-to-riches stories because we find something captivating in the idea of a lone hero battling overwhelming odds. But the true story of Joe Flom's life turns out to be much more intriguing than the mythological version because all the things in his life that seem to have been disadvantages—that he was a poor child of garment workers; that he was Jewish at a time when Jews were heavily discriminated against; that he grew up in the Depression—turn out, unexpectedly, to have been advantages. Joe Flom is an outlier. But he's not an outlier for the reasons you might think, and the story of his rise provides a blueprint for understanding success in his profession. By the end of the chapter, in fact, we'll see that it is possible to take the lessons of Joe Flom, apply them to the legal world of New York City, and predict the family background, age, and origin of the city's most powerful attorneys, *without knowing a single additional fact about them.* But we're getting ahead of ourselves.

Lesson Number One: The Importance of Being Jewish

3.

One of Joe Flom's classmates at Harvard Law School was a man named Alexander Bickel. Like Flom, Bickel was the son of Eastern European Jewish immigrants who lived in the Bronx. Like Flom, Bickel had gone to public school in New York and then to City College. Like Flom, Bickel was a star in his law school class. In fact, before his career was cut short by cancer, Bickel would become perhaps the finest constitutional scholar of his generation. And like Flom and the rest of their law school classmates, Bickel went to Manhattan during "hiring season" over Christmas of 1947 to find himself a job.

His first stop was at Mudge Rose, down on Wall Street, as traditional and stuffy as any firm of that era. Mudge Rose was founded in 1869. It was where Richard Nixon practiced in the years before he won the presidency in 1968. "We're like the lady who only wants her name in the newspaper twice—when she's born and when she dies," one of the senior partners famously said. Bickel was taken around the firm and interviewed by one partner after another, until he was led into the library to meet with the firm's senior partner. You can imagine the scene: a dark-paneled room, an artfully frayed Persian carpet, row upon row of leather-bound legal volumes, oil paintings of Mr. Mudge and Mr. Rose on the wall.

"After they put me through the whole interview and everything," Bickel said many years later, "I was brought to [the senior partner], who took it upon himself to tell me that for a boy of my *antecedents*"—and you can imagine how Bickel must have paused before repeating that euphemism for his immigrant background—"I certainly had come far. But I ought to understand how limited the possibilities of a firm like his were to hire a boy of my *antecedents*. And while he congratulated me on my progress, I should understand he certainly couldn't offer me a job. But they all enjoyed seeing me and all that."

It is clear from the transcript of Bickel's reminiscences that his interviewer does not quite know what to do with that information. Bickel was by the time of the interview at the height of his reputation. He had argued a case before the Supreme Court. He had written brilliant books. Mudge Rose saying no to Bickel because of his "antecedents" was like the Chicago Bulls turning down Michael Jordan because they were uncomfortable with black kids from North Carolina. It didn't make any sense.

"But for stars?" the interviewer asked, meaning, Wouldn't they have made an exception for *you?*

Bickel: "Stars, schmars…"

In the 1940s and 1950s, the old-line law firms of New York operated like a private club. They were all headquartered in downtown Manhattan, in and around Wall Street, in somber, granite-faced buildings. The partners at the top firms graduated from the same Ivy League schools, attended the same churches, and summered in the same oceanside towns on Long Island. They wore conservative gray suits. Their partnerships were known as "white-shoe" firms— in apparent reference to the white bucks favored at the country club or a cocktail party, and they were very particular in whom they hired. As Erwin Smigel wrote in *The Wall Street Lawyer,* his study of the New York legal establishment of that era, they were looking for:

lawyers who are Nordic, have pleasing personalities and "clean-cut" appearances, are graduates of the "right schools," have the "right" social background and experience in the affairs of the world, and are endowed with tremendous stamina. A former law school dean, in discussing the qualities students need to obtain a job, offers a somewhat more realistic picture: "To get a job [students] should be long enough on family connections, long enough on ability or long enough on personality, or a combination of these. Something called acceptability is made up of the sum of its parts. If a man has any of these things, he could get a job. If he has two of them, he can have a choice of jobs; if he has three, he could go anywhere."

Bickel's hair was not fair. His eyes were not blue. He spoke with an accent, and his family connections consisted, principally, of being the son of Solomon and Yetta Bickel of Bucharest, Romania, by way, most recently, of Brooklyn. Flom's credentials were no better. He says he felt "uncomfortable" when he went for his interviews downtown, and of course he did: he was short and ungainly and Jewish and talked with the flat, nasal tones of his native Brooklyn, and you can imagine how he would have been perceived by some silver-haired patrician in the library. If you were not of the right background and religion and social class and you came out of law school in that era, you joined some smaller, second-rate, upstart law firm on a rung below the big names downtown, or you simply went into business for yourself and took "whatever came in the door"— that is, whatever legal work the big downtown firms did not want for themselves. That seems horribly unfair, and it was. But as is so often the case with outliers, buried in that setback was a golden opportunity.

4.

The old-line Wall Street law firms had a very specific idea about what it was that they did. They were corporate lawyers. They represented the country's largest and most prestigious companies, and "represented" meant they handled the taxes and the legal work behind the issuing of stocks and bonds and made sure their clients did not run afoul of federal regulators. They did not do litigation; that is, very few of them had a division dedicated to defending and filing lawsuits. As Paul Cravath, one of the founders of Cravath, Swaine and Moore, the very whitest of the white-shoe firms, once put it, the lawyer's job was to settle disputes in the conference room, not in the courtroom. "Among my classmates at Harvard, the thing that bright young guys did was securities work or tax," another white-shoe partner remembers. "Those were the distinguished fields. Litigation was for hams, not for serious people. Corporations just didn't sue each other in those days."

What the old-line firms also did not do was involve themselves in hostile corporate takeovers. It's hard to imagine today, when corporate raiders and private-equity firms are constantly swallowing up one company after another, but until the 1970s, it was considered scandalous for one company to buy another company without the target agreeing to be bought. Places like Mudge Rose and the other establishment firms on Wall Street would not touch those kinds of deals.

"The problem with hostile takeovers is that they were hostile," says Steven Brill, who founded the trade magazine *American Lawyer*. "It wasn't gentlemanly. If your best buddy from Princeton is the CEO of Company X, and he's been coasting for a long time, and some corporate raider shows up and says this company sucks, it makes you uncomfortable. You think, If he goes, then maybe I go too. It's this whole notion of not upsetting the basic calm and stable order of things."[*]

The work that "came in the door" to the generation of Jewish lawyers from the Bronx and Brooklyn in the 1950s and 1960s, then, was the work the white-shoe firms disdained: litigation and, more important, "proxy fights," which were the legal maneuvers at the center of any hostile-takeover bid. An investor would take an interest in a company; he would denounce the management as incompetent and send letters to shareholders, trying to get them to give him their "proxy" so he could vote out the firm's executives. And to run the proxy fight, the only lawyer the investor could get was someone like Joe Flom.

In *Skadden*, the legal historian Lincoln Caplan describes that early world of takeovers:

> The winner of a proxy contest was determined in the snake pit. (Officially, it was called the counting room.) Lawyers for each side met with inspectors of elections, whose job it was to approve or eliminate questionable proxies. The event was often informal, contentious and unruly. Adversaries were sometimes in T-shirts, eating watermelon or sharing a bottle of scotch. In rare cases, the results of the snake pit could swing the outcome of a contest and turn on a single ballot.
>
> Lawyers occasionally tried to fix an election by engineering the appointment of inspectors who were beholden to them; inspectors commonly smoked cigars provided by each side. Management's lawyer would contest the proxies of the insurgents ("I challenge this!") and vice versa.... Lawyers who prevailed in the snake pit excelled at winging it. There were lawyers who knew more about the rules of proxy contests, but no one was better in a fight than Joe Flom...
>
> Flom was fat (a hundred pounds overweight then, one lawyer said...), physically unattractive (to a partner, he resembled a frog), and indifferent to social niceties (he would fart in public or jab a cigar close to the face of

someone he was talking to, without apology). But in the judgment of colleagues and of some adversaries, his will to win was unsurpassed and he was often masterful.

The white-shoe law firms would call in Flom as well whenever some corporate raider made a run at one of their establishment clients. They wouldn't touch the case. But they were happy to outsource it to Skadden, Arps. "Flom's early specialty was proxy fights, and that was not what we did, just like we don't do matrimonial work," said Robert Rifkind, a longtime partner at Cravath, Swaine and Moore. "And therefore we purported not to know about it. I remember once we had an issue involving a proxy fight, and one of my senior corporate partners said, Well, let's get Joe in. And he came to a conference room, and we all sat around and described the problem and he told us what to do and he left. And I said, 'We can do that too, you know.' And the partner said, 'No, no, no, you can't. We're not going to do that.' It was just that we didn't do it."

Then came the 1970s. The old aversion to lawsuits fell by the wayside. It became easier to borrow money. Federal regulations were relaxed. Markets became internationalized. Investors became more aggressive, and the result was a boom in the number and size of corporate takeovers. "In nineteen eighty, if you went to the Business Roundtable [the association of major American corporate executives] and took surveys about whether hostile takeovers should be allowed, two-thirds would have said no," Flom said. "Now, the vote would be almost unanimously yes." Companies needed to be defended against lawsuits from rivals. Hostile suitors needed to be beaten back. Investors who wanted to devour unwilling targets needed help with their legal strategy, and shareholders needed formal representation. The dollar figures involved were enormous. From the mid-1970s to the end of the 1980s, the amount of money involved in mergers and acquisitions every year on Wall Street increased *2,000 percent*, peaking at almost a quarter of a trillion dollars.

All of a sudden the things that the old-line law firms didn't want to do— hostile takeovers and litigation—were the things that *every* law firm wanted to do. And who was the expert in these two suddenly critical areas of law? The once marginal, second-tier law firms started by the people who couldn't get jobs at the downtown firms ten and fifteen years earlier.

"[The white-shoe firms] thought hostile takeovers were beneath contempt until relatively late in the game, and until they decided that, hey, maybe we ought to be in that business, they left me alone," Flom said. "And once you get the reputation for doing that kind of work, the business comes to you first."

Think of how similar this is to the stories of Bill Joy and Bill Gates. Both of them toiled away in a relatively obscure field without any great hopes for worldly success. But then—boom!—the personal computer revolution happened, and they had their ten thousand hours in. They were ready. Flom had the same experience. For twenty years he perfected his craft at Skadden, Arps. Then the world changed and he was ready. He didn't triumph over adversity. Instead, what started out as adversity ended up being an opportunity.

"It's not that those guys were smarter lawyers than anyone else," Rifkind says. "It's that they had a skill that they had been working on for years that was suddenly very valuable."[*]

Lesson Number Two: Demographic Luck

5.

Maurice Janklow enrolled in Brooklyn Law School in 1919. He was the eldest son of Jewish immigrants from Romania. He had seven brothers and sisters. One ended up running a small department store in Brooklyn. Two others were in the haberdashery business, one had a graphic design studio, another made feather hats, and another worked in the finance department at Tishman Realty.

Maurice, however, was the family intellectual, the only one to go to college. He got his law degree and set up a practice on Court Street in downtown Brooklyn. He was an elegant man who dressed in a homburg and Brooks Brothers suits. In the summer, he wore a straw boater. He married the very beautiful Lillian Levantin, who was the daughter of a prominent Talmudist. He drove a big car. He moved to Queens. He and a partner then took over a writing-paper business that gave every indication of making a fortune.

Here was a man who looked, for all the world, like the kind of person who should thrive as a lawyer in New York City. He was intelligent and educated. He came from a family well schooled in the rules of the system. He was living in the most economically vibrant city in the world. But here is the strange thing: it never happened. Maurice Janklow's career did not take off the way that he'd hoped. In his mind, he never really made it beyond Court Street in Brooklyn. He struggled and floundered.

Maurice Janklow had a son named Mort, however, who became a lawyer as well, and the son's story is very different from that of the father. Mort Janklow built a law firm from scratch in the 1960s, then put together one of the very earliest cable television franchises and sold it for a fortune to Cox Broadcasting. He started a literary agency in the 1970s, and it is today one of the most prestigious in the world.[*] He has his own plane. Every dream that eluded the father was fulfilled by the son.

Why did Mort Janklow succeed where Maurice Janklow did not? There are, of course, a hundred potential answers to that question. But let's take a page from the analysis of the business tycoons born in the 1830s and the software programmers born in 1955 and look at the differences between the two Janklows in terms of their generation. Is there a perfect time for a New York Jewish lawyer to be born? It turns out there is, and this same fact that helps explain Mort Janklow's success is the second key to Joe Flom's success as well.

6.

Lewis Terman's genius study, as you will recall from the chapter about Chris Langan, was an investigation into how some children with really high IQs who were born between 1903 and 1917 turned out as adults. And the study found that there was a group of real successes and there was a group of real failures, and that the successes were far more likely to have come from wealthier families. In that sense, the Terman study underscores the argument Annette Lareau makes, that what your parents do for a living, and the assumptions that accompany the class your parents belong to, *matter*.

There's another way to break down the Terman results, though, and that's by *when* the Termites were born. If you divide the Termites into two groups, with those born between 1903 and 1911 on one side, and those between 1912 and 1917 on the other, it turns out that the Terman failures are far more likely to have been born in the earlier group.

The explanation has to do with two of the great cataclysmic events of the twentieth century: the Great Depression and World War II. If you were born after 1912—say, in 1915—you got out of college after the worst of the Depression was over, and you were drafted at a young enough age that going away to war for three or four years was as much an opportunity as it was a disruption (provided you weren't killed, of course).

The Termites born before 1911, though, graduated from college at the height of the Depression, when job opportunities were scarce, and they were already in their late thirties when the Second World War hit, meaning that when they were drafted, they had to disrupt careers and families and adult lives that were already well under way. To have been born before 1911 is to have been demographically unlucky. The most devastating events of the twentieth century hit you at exactly the wrong time.

This same demographic logic applies to Jewish lawyers in New York like Maurice Janklow. The doors were closed to them at the big downtown law firms. So they were overwhelmingly solo practitioners, handling wills and divorces and contracts and minor disputes, and in the Depression the work of the solo practitioner all but disappeared. "Nearly half of the members of the metropolitan bar earned less than the minimum subsistence level for American families," Jerold Auerbach writes of the Depression years in New York. "One year later 1,500 lawyers were prepared to take the pauper's oath to qualify for work relief. Jewish lawyers (approximately one-half of the metropolitan bar) discovered that their practice had become a 'dignified road to starvation.' " Regardless of the number of years they had spent in practice, their income was "strikingly less" than that of their Christian colleagues. Maurice Janklow was born in 1902. When the Depression started, he was newly married and had just bought his big car, moved to Queens, and made his great gamble on the writing-paper business. His timing could not have been worse.

"He was going to make a fortune," Mort Janklow says of his father. "But the Depression killed him economically. He didn't have any reserves, and he had no family to fall back on. And from then on, he became very much a scrivener-type lawyer. He didn't have the courage to take risks after that. It was too much for him. My father used to close titles for twenty-five dollars. He had a friend who worked at the Jamaica Savings Bank who would throw him some business. He would kill himself for twenty-five bucks, doing the whole closing, title reports. For twenty-five bucks!

"I can remember my father and mother in the morning," Janklow continued. "He would say to her, 'I got a dollar seventy-five. I need ten cents for the bus, ten cents for the subway, a quarter for a sandwich,' and he would give her the rest. They were that close to the edge."

7.

Now contrast that experience with the experience of someone who, like Mort Janklow, was born in the 1930s.

Take a look at the following chart, which shows the birthrates in the United States from 1910 to 1950. In 1915, there are almost three million babies. In 1935, that number drops by almost six hundred thousand, and then, within a decade and a half, the number is back over three million again. To put it in more precise terms, for every thousand Americans, there were 29.5 babies born in 1915; 18.7 babies born in 1935; and 24.1 babies born in 1950. The decade of the 1930s is what is called a "demographic trough." In response to the economic hardship of the Depression, families simply stopped having children, and as a result, the generation born during that decade was markedly smaller than both the generation that preceded it and the generation that immediately followed it.

Year	Total Births	Births per 1
1910	2,777,000	30.1
1915	2,965,000	29.5
1920	2,950,000	27.7
1925	2,909,000	25.1
1930	2,618,000	21.3
1935	2,377,000	18.7
1940	2,559,000	19.4
1945	2,858,000	20.4
1950	3,632,000	24.1

Here is what the economist H. Scott Gordon once wrote about the particular benefits of being one of those people born in a small generation:

When he opens his eyes for the first time, it is in a spacious hospital, well-appointed to serve the wave that preceded him. The staff is generous with their time, since they have little to do while they ride out the brief period of calm until the next wave hits. When he comes to school age, the magnificent buildings are already there to receive him; the ample staff of teachers welcomes him with open arms. In high school, the basketball team is not as good as it was but there is no problem getting time on the gymnasium floor. The university is a delightful place; lots of room in the classes and residences, no crowding in the cafeteria, and the professors are solicitous. Then he hits the job market. The supply of new entrants is low, and the demand is high, because there is a large wave coming behind him providing a strong demand for the goods and services of his potential employers.

In New York City, the early 1930s cohort was so small that class sizes were at least half of what they had been twenty-five years earlier. The schools were new, built for the big generation that had come before, and the teachers had what in the Depression was considered a high-status job.

"The New York City public schools of the 1940s were considered the best schools in the country," says Diane Ravitch, a professor at New York University who has written widely on the city's educational history. "There was this generation of educators in the thirties and forties who would have been in another time and place college professors. They were brilliant, but they couldn't get the jobs they wanted, and public teaching was what they did because it was security and it had a pension and you didn't get laid off."

The same dynamic benefited the members of that generation when they went off to college. Here is Ted Friedman, one of the top litigators in New York in the 1970s and 1980s. Like Flom, he grew up poor, the child of struggling Jewish immigrants.

"My options were City College and the University of Michigan," Friedman said. City College was free, and Michigan—then, as now, one of the top universities in the United States—was $450 a year. "And the thing was, after the first year, you could get a scholarship if your grades were high," Friedman said. "So it was only the first year I had to pay that, if I did well." Friedman's first inclination was to stay in New York. "Well, I went to City College for one day, I didn't like it. I thought, This is going to be four more years of Bronx Science [the high school he had attended], and came home, packed my bags, and hitchhiked to Ann Arbor." He went on:

I had a couple of hundred dollars in my pocket from the summer. I was working the Catskills to make enough money to pay the four-hundred-fifty-dollar tuition, and I had some left over. Then there was this fancy restaurant in Ann Arbor where I got a job waiting tables. I also worked the night shift at River Rouge, the big Ford plant. That was real money. It wasn't so hard to get that job. The factories were looking for people. I had another job too, which paid me the best pay I ever had before I became a lawyer, which was working in construction. During the summer, in Ann Arbor, we built the Chrysler proving grounds. I worked there a few summers during law school. Those jobs were really high paying, probably because you worked so much overtime.

Think about this story for a moment. The first lesson is that Friedman was willing to work hard, take responsibility for himself, and put himself through school. But the second, perhaps more important lesson is that he happened to come along at a time in America when if you were willing to work hard, you *could* take responsibility for yourself and put yourself through school. Friedman was, at the time, what we would today call "economically disadvantaged." He was an inner-city kid from the Bronx, neither of whose parents went to college. But look at how easy it was for him to get a good education. He graduated from his public high school in New York at a time when New York City public schools were the envy of the world. His first option, City College, was free, and his second option, the University of Michigan, cost just $450—and the admissions process was casual enough, apparently, that he could try one school one day and the other the next.

And how did he get there? He hitchhiked, with the money that he made in the summer in his pocket, and when he arrived, he immediately got a series of really good jobs to help pay his way, because the factories were "looking for people." And of course they were: they had to feed the needs of the big generation just ahead of those born in the demographic trough of the 1930s, and the big generation of baby boomers coming up behind them. The sense of possibility so necessary for success comes not just from inside us or from our parents. It comes from our time: from the particular opportunities that our particular place in history presents us with. For a young would-be lawyer, being born in the early 1930s was a magic time, just as being born in 1955 was for a software programmer, or being born in 1835 was for an entrepreneur.

Today, Mort Janklow has an office high above Park Avenue filled with gorgeous works of modern art—a Dubuffet, an Anselm Kiefer. He tells hilarious stories. ("My mother had two sisters. One lived to be ninety-nine and the other died at ninety. The ninety-nine-year-old was a smart woman. She married my Uncle Al, who was the chief of sales for Maidenform. Once I said to him, 'What's the rest of the country like, Uncle Al?' And he said, 'Kiddo. When you leave New York, every place is Bridgeport.' ") He gives the sense that the world is his for the taking. "I've always been a big risk taker," he says. "When I built the cable company, in the early stages, I was making deals where I would have been bankrupt if I hadn't pulled it off. I had confidence that I could make it work."

Mort Janklow went to New York City public schools when they were at their best. Maurice Janklow went to New York City public schools when they were at their most overcrowded. Mort Janklow went to Columbia University Law School, because demographic trough babies have their pick of selective schools. Maurice Janklow went to Brooklyn Law School, which was as good as an immigrant child could do in 1919. Mort Janklow sold his cable business for tens of millions of dollars. Maurice Janklow closed titles for twenty-five dollars. The story of the Janklows tells us that the meteoric rise of Joe Flom could not have happened at just any time. Even the most gifted of lawyers, equipped with the best of family lessons, cannot escape the limitations of their generation.

"My mother was coherent until the last five or six months of her life," Mort Janklow said. "And in her delirium she talked about things that she'd never talked about before. She shed tears over her friends dying in the 1918 flu epidemic. That generation—my parents' generation—lived through a lot. They lived through that epidemic, which took, what? ten percent of the world's population. Panic in the streets. Friends dying. And then the First World War, then the Depression, then the Second World War. They didn't have much of a chance. That was a very tough period. My father would have been much more successful in a different kind of world."

Lesson Number Three: The Garment Industry and Meaningful Work

8.

In 1889, Louis and Regina Borgenicht boarded an ocean liner in Hamburg bound for America. Louis was from Galacia, in what was then Poland. Regina was from a small town in Hungary. They had been married only a few years and had one small child and a second on the way. For the thirteen-day journey, they slept on straw mattresses on a deck above the engine room, hanging tight to their bunk beds as the ship pitched and rolled. They knew one person in New York: Borgenicht's sister, Sallie, who had immigrated ten years before. They had enough money to last a few weeks, at best. Like so many other immigrants to America in those years, theirs was a leap of faith.

Louis and Regina found a tiny apartment on Eldridge Street, on Manhattan's Lower East Side, for $8 a month. Louis then took to the streets, looking for work. He saw peddlers and fruit sellers and sidewalks crammed with pushcarts. The noise and activity and energy dwarfed what he had known in the Old World. He was first overwhelmed, then invigorated. He went to his sister's fish store on Ludlow Street and persuaded her to give him a consignment of herring on credit. He set up shop on the sidewalk with two barrels of fish, hopping back and forth between them and chanting in German:

> For frying
> For baking
> For cooking
> Good also for eating
> Herring will do for every meal,
> And for every class!

By the end of the week, he had cleared $8. By the second week, $13. Those were considerable sums. But Louis and Regina could not see how selling herring on the street would lead to a constructive business. Louis then decided to try being a pushcart peddler. He sold towels and tablecloths, without much luck. He switched to notebooks, then bananas, then socks and stockings. Was there really a future in pushcarts? Regina gave birth to a second child, a daughter, and Louis's urgency grew. He now had four mouths to feed.

The answer came to him after five long days of walking up and down the streets of the Lower East Side, just as he was about to give up hope. He was sitting on an overturned box, eating a late lunch of the sandwiches Regina had made for him. *It was clothes.* Everywhere around him stores were opening— suits, dresses, overalls, shirts, skirts, blouses, trousers, all made and ready to be worn. Coming from a world where clothing was sewn at home by hand or made to order by tailors, this was a revelation.

"To me the greatest wonder in this was not the mere quantity of garments— although that was a miracle in itself—" Borgenicht would write years later, after he became a prosperous manufacturer of women's and children's clothing, "but the fact that in America even poor people could save all the dreary, time- consuming labor of making their own clothes simply by going into a store and walking out with what they needed. *There* was a field to go into, a field to thrill to."

Borgenicht took out a small notebook. Everywhere he went, he wrote down what people were wearing and what was for sale—menswear, women's wear, children's wear. He wanted to find a "novel" item, something that people would wear that was not being sold in the stores. For four more days he walked the streets. On the evening of the final day as he walked toward home, he saw a half dozen girls playing hopscotch. One of the girls was wearing a tiny embroidered apron over her dress, cut low in the front with a tie in the back, and it struck him, suddenly, that in his previous days of relentlessly inventorying the clothing shops of the Lower East Side, he had *never* seen one of those aprons for sale.

He came home and told Regina. She had an ancient sewing machine that they had bought upon their arrival in America. The next morning, he went to a dry-goods store on Hester Street and bought a hundred yards of gingham and fifty yards of white crossbar. He came back to their tiny apartment and laid the goods out on the dining room table. Regina began to cut the gingham—small sizes for toddlers, larger for small children—until she had forty aprons. She began to sew. At midnight, she went to bed and Louis took up where she had left off. At dawn, she rose and began cutting buttonholes and adding buttons. By ten in the morning, the aprons were finished. Louis gathered them up over his arm and ventured out onto Hester Street.

"Children's aprons! Little girls' aprons! Colored ones, ten cents. White ones, fifteen cents! Little girls' aprons!"

By one o'clock, all forty were gone.

"Ma, we've got our business," he shouted out to Regina, after running all the way home from Hester Street.

He grabbed her by the waist and began swinging her around and around.

"You've got to help me," he cried out. "We'll work together! Ma, *this is our business.*"

9.

Jewish immigrants like the Floms and the Borgenichts and the Janklows were not like the other immigrants who came to America in the nineteenth and early twentieth centuries. The Irish and the Italians were peasants, tenant farmers from the impoverished countryside of Europe. Not so the Jews. For centuries in

Europe, they had been forbidden to own land, so they had clustered in cities and towns, taking up urban trades and professions. Seventy percent of the Eastern European Jews who came through Ellis Island in the thirty years or so before the First World War had some kind of occupational skill. They had owned small groceries or jewelry stores. They had been bookbinders or watchmakers. Overwhelmingly, though, their experience lay in the clothing trade. They were tailors and dressmakers, hat and cap makers, and furriers and tanners.

Louis Borgenicht, for example, left the impoverished home of his parents at age twelve to work as a salesclerk in a general store in the Polish town of Brzesko. When the opportunity came to work in *Schnittwaren Handlung* (literally, the handling of cloth and fabrics or "piece goods," as they were known), he jumped at it. "In those days, the piece-goods man was clothier to the world," he writes, "and of the three fundamentals required for life in that simple society, food and shelter were humble. Clothing was the aristocrat. Practitioners of the clothing art, dealers in wonderful cloths from every corner of Europe, traders who visited the centers of industry on their annual buying tours—these were the merchant princes of my youth. Their voices were heard, their weight felt."

Borgenicht worked in piece goods for a man named Epstein, then moved on to a store in neighboring Jaslow called Brandstatter's. It was there that the young Borgenicht learned the ins and outs of all the dozens of different varieties of cloth, to the point where he could run his hand over a fabric and tell you the thread count, the name of the manufacturer, and its place of origin. A few years later, Borgenicht moved to Hungary and met Regina. She had been running a dressmaking business since the age of sixteen. Together they opened a series of small piece-goods stores, painstakingly learning the details of small-business entrepreneurship.

Borgenicht's great brainstorm that day on the upturned box, then, did not come from nowhere. He was a veteran of *Schnittwaren Handlung,* and his wife was a seasoned dressmaker. This was their field. And at the same time as the Borgenichts set up shop inside their tiny apartment, thousands of other Jewish immigrants were doing the same thing, putting their sewing and dressmaking and tailoring skills to use, to the point where by 1900, control of the garment industry had passed almost entirely into the hands of the Eastern European newcomers. As Borgenicht puts it, the Jews "bit deep into the welcoming land and worked like madmen *at what they knew.*"

Today, at a time when New York is at the center of an enormous and diversified metropolitan area, it is easy to forget the significance of the set of skills that immigrants like the Borgenichts brought to the New World. From the late nineteenth century through the middle of the twentieth century, the garment trade was the largest and most economically vibrant industry in the city. More people worked making clothes in New York than at anything else, and more clothes were manufactured in New York than in any other city in the world. The distinctive buildings that still stand on the lower half of Broadway in Manhattan —from the big ten- and fifteen-story industrial warehouses in the twenty blocks below Times Square to the cast-iron lofts of SoHo and Tribeca—were almost all built to house coat makers and hatmakers and lingerie manufacturers and huge rooms of men and women hunched over sewing machines. To come to New York City in the 1890s with a background in dressmaking or sewing or *Schnittwaren Handlung* was a stroke of extraordinary good fortune. It was like showing up in Silicon Valley in 1986 with ten thousand hours of computer programming already under your belt.

"There is no doubt that those Jewish immigrants arrived at the perfect time, with the perfect skills," says the sociologist Stephen Steinberg. "To exploit that opportunity, you had to have certain virtues, and those immigrants worked hard. They sacrificed. They scrimped and saved and invested wisely. But still, you have to remember that the garment industry in those years was growing by leaps and bounds. The economy was desperate for the skills that they possessed."

Louis and Regina Borgenicht and the thousands of others who came over on the boats with them were given a golden opportunity. And so were their children and grandchildren, because the lessons those garment workers brought home with them in the evenings turned out to be critical for getting ahead in the world.

10.

The day after Louis and Regina Borgenicht sold out their first lot of forty aprons, Louis made his way to H. B. Claflin and Company. Claflin was a dry-goods "commission" house, the equivalent of Brandstatter's back in Poland. There, Borgenicht asked for a salesman who spoke German, since his English was almost nonexistent. He had in his hand his and Regina's life savings—$12—and with that money, he bought enough cloth to make ten dozen aprons. Day and night, he and Regina cut and sewed. He sold all ten dozen in two days. Back he went to Claflin for another round. They sold those too. Before long, he and

Regina hired another immigrant just off the boat to help with the children so Regina could sew full-time, and then another to serve as an apprentice. Louis ventured uptown as far as Harlem, selling to the mothers in the tenements. He rented a storefront on Sheriff Street, with living quarters in the back. He hired three more girls, and bought sewing machines for all of them. He became known as "the apron man." He and Regina were selling aprons as fast as they could make them.

Before long, the Borgenichts decided to branch out. They started making adult aprons, then petticoats, then women's dresses. By January of 1892, the Borgenichts had twenty people working for them, mostly immigrant Jews like themselves. They had their own factory on the Lower East Side of Manhattan and a growing list of customers, including a store uptown owned by another Jewish immigrant family, the Bloomingdale brothers. Keep in mind the Borgenichts had been in the country for only three years at this point. They barely spoke English. And they weren't rich yet by any stretch of the imagination. Whatever profit they made got plowed back into their business, and Borgenicht says he had only $200 in the bank. But already he was in charge of his own destiny.

This was the second great advantage of the garment industry. It wasn't just that it was growing by leaps and bounds. It was also explicitly entrepreneurial. Clothes weren't made in a single big factory. Instead, a number of established firms designed patterns and prepared the fabric, and then the complicated stitching and pressing and button attaching were all sent out to small contractors. And if a contractor got big enough, or ambitious enough, he started designing his own patterns and preparing his own fabric. By 1913, there were approximately sixteen thousand separate companies in New York City's garment business, many just like the Borgenichts' shop on Sheriff Street.

"The threshold for getting involved in the business was very low. It's basically a business built on the sewing machine, and sewing machines don't cost that much," says Daniel Soyer, a historian who has written widely on the garment industry. "So you didn't need a lot of capital. At the turn of the twentieth century, it was probably fifty dollars to buy a machine or two. All you had to do to be a contractor was to have a couple sewing machines, some irons, and a couple of workers. The profit margins were very low but you could make some money."

Listen to how Borgenicht describes his decision to expand beyond aprons:

From my study of the market I knew that only three men were making children's dresses in 1890. One was an East Side tailor near me, who made only to order, while the other two turned out an expensive product with which I had no desire at all to compete. I wanted to make "popular price" stuff—wash dresses, silks, and woolens. It was my goal to produce dresses that the great mass of the people could afford, dresses that would —from the business angle—sell equally well to both large and small, city and country stores. With Regina's help—she always had excellent taste, and judgment—I made up a line of samples. Displaying them to all my "old" customers and friends, I hammered home every point—my dresses would save mothers endless work, the materials and sewing were as good and probably better than anything that could be done at home, the price was right for quick disposal.

On one occasion, Borgenicht realized that his only chance to undercut bigger firms was to convince the wholesalers to sell cloth to him directly, eliminating the middleman. He went to see a Mr. Bingham at Lawrence and Company, a "tall, gaunt, white-bearded Yankee with steel-blue eyes." There the two of them were, the immigrant from rural Poland, his eyes ringed with fatigue, facing off in his halting English against the imperious Yankee. Borgenicht said he wanted to buy forty cases of cashmere. Bingham had never before sold to an individual company, let alone a shoestring operation on Sheriff Street.

"You have a hell of a cheek coming in here and asking me for favors!" Bingham thundered. But he ended up saying yes.

What Borgenicht was getting in his eighteen-hour days was a lesson in the modern economy. He was learning market research. He was learning manufacturing. He was learning how to negotiate with imperious Yankees. He was learning how to plug himself into popular culture in order to understand new fashion trends.

The Irish and Italian immigrants who came to New York in the same period didn't have that advantage. They didn't have a skill specific to the urban economy. They went to work as day laborers and domestics and construction workers—jobs where you could show up for work every day for thirty years and never learn market research and manufacturing and how to navigate the popular culture and how to negotiate with the Yankees, who ran the world.

Or consider the fate of the Mexicans who immigrated to California between

1900 and the end of the 1920s to work in the fields of the big fruit and vegetable growers. They simply exchanged the life of a feudal peasant in Mexico for the life of a feudal peasant in California. "The conditions in the garment industry were every bit as bad," Soyer goes on. "But as a garment worker, you were closer to the center of the industry. If you are working in a field in California, you have no clue what's happening to the produce when it gets on the truck. If you are working in a small garment shop, your wages are low, and your conditions are terrible, and your hours are long, but you can see exactly what the successful people are doing, and you can see how you can set up your own job."[*]

When Borgenicht came home at night to his children, he may have been tired and poor and overwhelmed, but he was alive. He was his own boss. He was responsible for his own decisions and direction. His work was complex: it engaged his mind and imagination. And in his work, there was a relationship between effort and reward: the longer he and Regina stayed up at night sewing aprons, the more money they made the next day on the streets.

Those three things—autonomy, complexity, and a connection between effort and reward—are, most people agree, the three qualities that work has to have if it is to be satisfying. It is not how much money we make that ultimately makes us happy between nine and five. It's whether our work fulfills us. If I offered you a choice between being an architect for $75,000 a year and working in a tollbooth every day for the rest of your life for $100,000 a year, which would you take? I'm guessing the former, because there is complexity, autonomy, and a relationship between effort and reward in doing creative work, and that's worth more to most of us than money.

Work that fulfills those three criteria is *meaningful*. Being a teacher is meaningful. Being a physician is meaningful. So is being an entrepreneur, and the miracle of the garment industry—as cutthroat and grim as it was—was that it allowed people like the Borgenichts, just off the boat, to find something meaningful to do as well.[*] When Louis Borgenicht came home after first seeing that child's apron, he danced a jig. He hadn't sold anything yet. He was still penniless and desperate, and he knew that to make something of his idea was going to require years of backbreaking labor. But he was ecstatic, because the prospect of those endless years of hard labor did not seem like a burden to him. Bill Gates had that same feeling when he first sat down at the keyboard at Lakeside. And the Beatles didn't recoil in horror when they were told they had to play eight hours a night, seven days a week. They jumped at the chance. Hard work is a prison sentence only if it does not have meaning. Once it does, it becomes the kind of thing that makes you grab your wife around the waist and dance a jig.

The most important consequence of the miracle of the garment industry, though, was what happened to the children growing up in those homes where meaningful work was practiced. Imagine what it must have been like to watch the meteoric rise of Regina and Louis Borgenicht through the eyes of one of their offspring. They learned the same lesson that little Alex Williams would learn nearly a century later—a lesson crucial to those who wanted to tackle the upper reaches of a profession like law or medicine: if you work hard enough and assert yourself, and use your mind and imagination, you can shape the world to your desires.

11.

In 1982, a sociology graduate student named Louise Farkas went to visit a number of nursing homes and residential hotels in New York City and Miami Beach. She was looking for people like the Borgenichts, or, more precisely, the children of people like the Borgenichts, who had come to New York in the great wave of Jewish immigration at the turn of the last century. And for each of the people she interviewed, she constructed a family tree showing what a line of parents and children and grandchildren and, in some cases, great-grandchildren did for a living.

Here is her account of "subject #18":

A Russian tailor artisan comes to America, takes to the needle trade, works in a sweat shop for a small salary. Later takes garments to finish at home with the help of his wife and older children. In order to increase his salary he works through the night. Later he makes a garment and sells it on New York streets. He accumulates some capital and goes into a business venture with his sons. They open a shop to create men's garments. The Russian tailor and his sons become men's suit manufacturers supplying several men's stores…. The sons and the father become prosperous…. The sons' children become educated professionals.

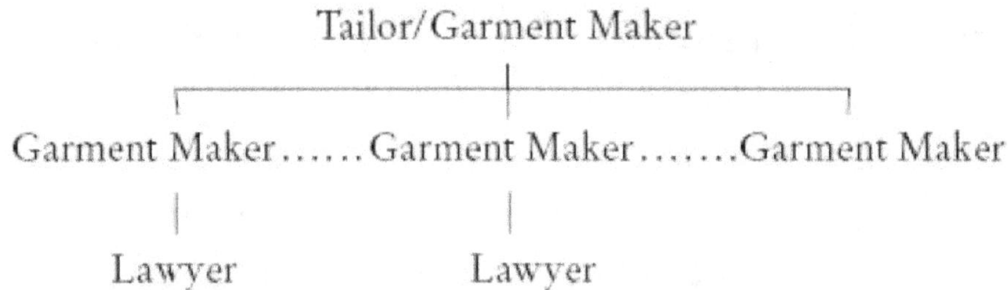

Here's another. It's a tanner who emigrated from Poland in the late nineteenth century.

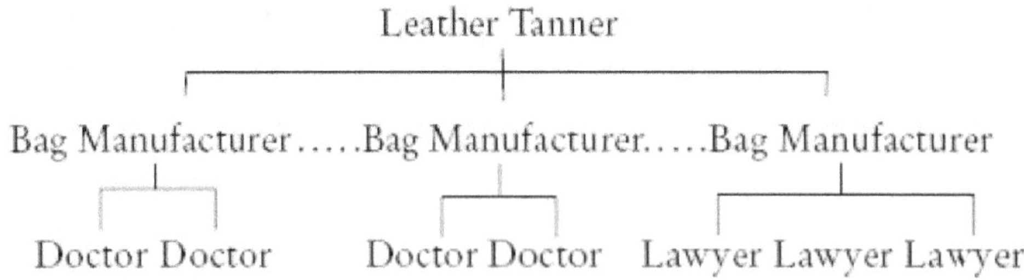

Farkas's Jewish family trees go on for pages, each virtually identical to the one before, until the conclusion becomes inescapable: Jewish doctors and lawyers did not become professionals in spite of their humble origins. They became professionals *because* of their humble origins.

Ted Friedman, the prominent litigator in the 1970s and 1980s, remembers as a child going to concerts with his mother at Carnegie Hall. They were poor and living in the farthest corners of the Bronx. How did they afford tickets? "Mary got a quarter," Friedman says. "There was a Mary who was a ticket taker, and if you gave Mary a quarter, she would let you stand in the second balcony, without a ticket. Carnegie Hall didn't know about it. It was just between you and Mary. It was a bit of a journey, but we would go back once or twice a month."[*]

Friedman's mother was a Russian immigrant. She barely spoke English. But she had gone to work as a seamstress at the age of fifteen and had become a prominent garment union organizer, and what you learn in that world is that through your own powers of persuasion and initiative, you can take your kids to Carnegie Hall. There is no better lesson for a budding lawyer than that. The garment industry was boot camp for the professions.

What did Joe Flom's father do? He sewed shoulder pads for women's dresses. What did Robert Oppenheimer's father do? He was a garment manufacturer, like Louis Borgenicht. One flight up from Flom's corner office at Skadden, Arps is the office of Barry Garfinkel, who has been at Skadden, Arps nearly as long as Flom and who for many years headed the firm's litigation department. What did Garfinkel's mother do? She was a milliner. She made hats at home. What did two of Louis and Regina Borgenicht's sons do? They went to law school, and no less than nine of their grandchildren ended up as doctors and lawyers as well.

Here is the most remarkable of Farkas's family trees. It belongs to a Jewish family from Romania who had a small grocery store in the Old Country and then came to New York and opened another, on the Lower East Side of Manhattan. It is the most elegant answer to the question of where all the Joe Floms came from.

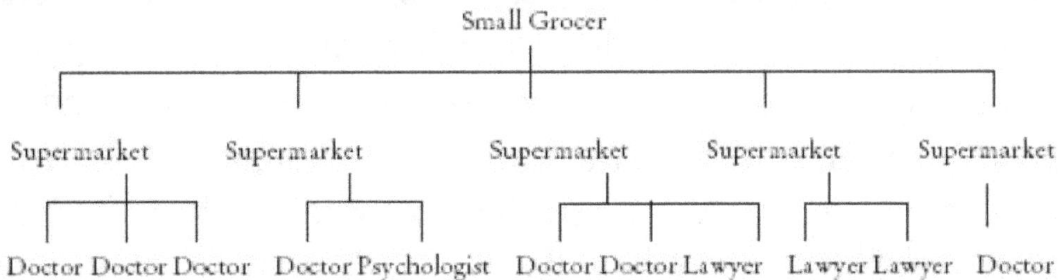

12.

Ten blocks north of the Skadden, Arps headquarters in midtown Manhattan are the offices of Joe Flom's great rival, the law firm generally regarded as the finest in the world.

It is headquartered in the prestigious office building known as Black Rock. To get hired there takes a small miracle. Unlike New York's other major law firms, all of which have hundreds of attorneys scattered around the major capitals of the world, it operates only out of that single Manhattan building. It turns down much more business than it accepts. Unlike every one of its competitors, it does not bill by the hour. It simply names a fee. Once, while defending Kmart against a takeover, the firm billed $20 million for two weeks' work. Kmart paid—happily. If its attorneys do not outsmart you, they will outwork you, and if they can't outwork you, they'll win through sheer intimidation. There is no firm in the world that has made more money, lawyer for lawyer, over the past two decades. On Joe Flom's wall, next to pictures of Flom with George Bush Sr. and Bill Clinton, there is a picture of him with the rival firm's managing partner.

No one rises to the top of the New York legal profession unless he or she is smart and ambitious and hardworking, and clearly the four men who founded the Black Rock firm fit that description. But we know far more than that, don't we? Success is not a random act. It arises out of a predictable and powerful set of circumstances and opportunities, and at this point, after examining the lives of

Bill Joy and Bill Gates, pro hockey players and geniuses, and Joe Flom, the Janklows, and the Borgenichts, it shouldn't be hard to figure out where the perfect lawyer comes from.

This person will have been born in a demographic trough, so as to have had the best of New York's public schools and the easiest time in the job market. He will be Jewish, of course, and so, locked out of the old-line downtown law firms on account of his "antecedents." This person's parents will have done meaningful work in the garment business, passing on to their children autonomy and complexity and the connection between effort and reward. A good school— although it doesn't have to be a great school—will have been attended. He need not have been the smartest in the class, only smart enough.

In fact, we can be even more precise. Just as there is a perfect birth date for a nineteenth-century business tycoon, and a perfect birth date for a software tycoon, there is a perfect birth date for a New York Jewish lawyer as well. It's 1930, because that would give the lawyer the benefit of a blessedly small generation. It would also make him forty years of age in 1970, when the revolution in the legal world first began, which translates to a healthy fifteen-year Hamburg period in the takeover business while the white-shoe lawyers lingered, oblivious, over their two-martini lunches. If you want to be a great New York lawyer, it is an advantage to be an outsider, and it is an advantage to have parents who did meaningful work, and, better still, it is an advantage to have been born in the early 1930s. But if you have all three advantages—on top of a good dose of ingenuity and drive—then that's an unstoppable combination. That's like being a hockey player born on January 1.

The Black Rock law firm is Wachtell, Lipton, Rosen & Katz. The firm's first partner was Herbert Wachtell. He was born in 1931. He grew up in the Amalgamated Clothing Workers union housing across from Van Cortlandt Park, in the Bronx. His parents were Jewish immigrants from the Ukraine. His father was in the ladies' undergarment business with his brothers, on the sixth floor of what is now a fancy loft at Broadway and Spring Street in SoHo. He went to New York City public schools in the 1940s, then to New York University, and then to New York University Law School.

The second partner was Martin Lipton. He was born in 1931. His father was a manager at a factory. He was a descendant of Jewish immigrants. He attended public schools in Jersey City, then the University of Pennsylvania, then New York University Law School.

The third partner was Leonard Rosen. He was born in 1930. He grew up poor in the Bronx, near Yankee Stadium. His parents were Jewish immigrants from the Ukraine. His father worked in the garment district in Manhattan as a presser. He went to New York City public schools in the 1940s, then to City College in upper Manhattan, and then to New York University Law School.

The fourth partner was George Katz. He was born in 1931. He grew up in a one-bedroom first-floor apartment in the Bronx. His parents were the children of Jewish immigrants from Eastern Europe. His father sold insurance. His grandfather, who lived a few blocks away, was a sewer in the garment trade, doing piecework out of his house. He went to New York City public schools in the 1940s, then to City College in upper Manhattan, and then to New York University Law School.

Imagine that we had met any one of these four fresh out of law school, sitting in the elegant waiting room at Mudge Rose next to a blue-eyed Nordic type from the "right" background. We'd all have bet on the Nordic type. And we would have been wrong, because the Katzes and the Rosens and the Liptons and the Wachtells and the Floms had something that the Nordic type did not. Their world —their culture and generation and family history—gave them the greatest of opportunities.